Collins

Enhanced Engaging English 7

Workbook

Name: ____________________

Grade: ________ Section: __________

Preeti Roychoudhury
Sadeqa Rahman Siddiqui

HarperCollins*Publishers*

Publishing operations in 17 countries and 120+ imprints globally

William Collins' dream of knowledge for all began with the publication of his first book in 1819. A self-educated mill worker, he not only enriched millions of lives, but also founded a flourishing publishing house. Today, staying true to this spirit, Collins books are packed with inspiration, innovation and practical expertise. They place you at the centre of a world of possibility and give you exactly what you need to explore it.

Published by Collins Learning
An imprint of HarperCollins*Publishers* India
Building No. 10, Tower A, 4th Floor, DLF Cyber City, Gurugram, Haryana 122002, India

Revised edition: 2025
Reprint: 10 9 8 7 6 5 4 3 2 1
ISBN: 978-93-6569-734-6
Printed and bound in India by MicroPrints India, New Delhi

Browse the complete Collins catalogue at www.collins.in.
For any queries/feedback, please write to us at SCHOOLSUPPORT@harpercollins.co.in.

Preface

Enhanced Engaging English aims to instill an appreciation for literature in today's learners, while equipping them with the tools to develop native fluency and communicative competence in using the English language. The eight-level series comprises Coursebooks, Workbooks, and digital resources for teachers for all levels.

The revised edition has been aligned closely with the guidelines of the National Curriculum Framework, 2023 through its focus on twenty-first century skills, Sustainable Development Goals (SDGs), cross-curricular learning, 'Happiness' content and art-integrated learning. Coursebooks and Workbooks 1 and 2 integrate the essence of NIPUN (National Initiative for Proficiency in Reading with Understanding and Numeracy). They aim to motivate students to read independently, improve their vocabulary, develop their critical thinking and creative skills and enhance their ability to express themselves verbally and in writing.

The lessons are built around carefully selected literary pieces with distinct cross-curricular themes, and presented with glossary, explanation of literary terms and interesting trivia. The end-of-chapter exercises address the needs of formal language learning.

The **Workbooks** are designed to complement the Coursebooks, by providing additional skills practice, review and assessments. They comprise the following sections:

Comprehension includes factual, inferential and evaluative questions based on short reading passages.

Way with Words includes exercises on the vocabulary topics encountered in the Coursebook as well as extension activities derived from it. It also incorporates activities on literary devices and figures of speech, spelling drills and exercises on dictionary usage.

Grammar in Use starts with a short explanation of important grammar concepts covered in the Coursebook, followed by plenty of practice for reinforcement.

Listening and Speaking builds students' oral and aural communication skills. It includes tasks such as phonics drills, conversation practice, role plays and debates to develop spoken English skills. Listening comprehension exercises teach students to listen for both general and specific details. In poetry chapters, there are activities on stress, rhyme and metre.

Pen it Down: The activities in this section include guided and free writing tasks derived from the reading text, which build on the functional and creative writing skills of the learner.

Each Workbook also contains two **Tests**. One of these is based on the principle of SAFAL (Structured Assessment For Analyzing Learning), a competency-based assessment introduced by CBSE. They assess the competencies of critical thinking as well as inquiry-based and analysis-based learning. The other test is modelled on class assessments.

The series encourages competency-based education which allows concept acquisition at the learner's own pace, based on individual ability. We hope that it will foster a love for literature and reading in young learners.

Detailed Contents

Unit	Theme	Way with Words	Grammar in Use	Listening and Speaking	Pen it Down
1. Three Questions	Neighbourhood and Community	• Forming words using prefixes and suffixes • Synonyms	• Transitive and intransitive verbs • Using *few/a few, little/a little, little/less*	• Conversation using close-ended and open-ended questions	• Email writing
2. Hope is the Thing with Feathers	Selfhood	• Imagery	• Determiners • Phrases and clauses	• Listening comprehension: answering questions • Debate on a given topic	• Message writing • Paragraph writing
3. Looking for Vultures' Eggs	Adventure and Imagination	• Collocations • Word association	• Converting adjectives to nouns • Transformation of sentences: interrogative and assertive	• Describing a scene • Speaking on a given topic	• Writing on a given topic • Writing alternate ending to a story
4. Coromandel Fishers	Professions	• Idioms	• Transformation of sentences: exclamatory and assertive	• Recitation	• Essay writing
5. Where Tigers Swim	Endangered Animals	• Compound adjectives • Commonly confused words	• Types of adjectives • Tenses	• Listening comprehension: true/false • Research and presentation on a given topic	• Essay writing
6. Composed upon Westminster Bridge, September 3, 1802	Tales of the City	• Simile • Personification	• Perfect and perfect continuous tense • Punctuation • Apostrophe	• Conversation: expressing admiration • Stressed syllables	• Email writing • Picture composition
7. Mary Shelley	Creatures of the Dark	• Word meanings • Forming antonyms with prefixes	• Adjective and noun phrases • Transformation of sentences with adjective phrases	• Speaking on a given topic	• Writing a notice
8. Grannie	Family	• Emotive language • Phrasal verbs with *stand* and *back*	• Question tags • Comparison of adjectives	• Rhyme scheme • Debate on a given topic	• Making a poster
9. Grandpa Learns to Read and Write	Books and Reading	• Crossword • Idioms	• Prepositions • Prepositional phrases	• Group discussion and giving a short speech	• Informal letter
Test Paper					

Unit	Theme	Way with Words	Grammar in Use	Listening and Speaking	Pen it Down
10. Dar es Salaam to Nairobi by Ford Prefect	Travel	• Onomatopoeia • Word search	• Infinitives • Transformation of sentences using infinitives • Gerunds	• Listening comprehension: answering questions	• Formal letter
11. Uncle Alfred's Long Jump	Humour	• Irony • Proverbs	• Coordinating and subordinating conjunctions • Indefinite pronouns	• Class discussion on a given topic	• Writing a report
12. The Invisible Man	Science Fiction	• Figurative language • Nominalisation	• Present and past participles • Active and passive voice	• Conversation: asking for help	• Essay writing
13. The Model Millionaire	Art and Culture	• Antonyms • Contextual usage	• Modals • Transformation of sentences using *if* and *unless*	• Conversation: speaking on given topics	• Diary entry
14. The Human Seasons	Cycle of Life	• Idioms	• Main and subordinate clauses	• Rising and falling intonation	• Writing a poem
15. Miss Smith and the Black Pearl	Race and the Arts	• Homographs • Homonyms • Making sentences	• Simple, compound and complex sentences • Adjective clauses	• Conversation: speaking on a given topic	• Writing a letter
16. Unbreakable	Women in Sports	• Expressions related to sports	• Noun and adverb clauses	• Enacting an interview	• Picture composition
17. At the Theatre: To the Lady Behind Me	On the Stage	• Idioms with *play* • Collective nouns	• Position of adverbs • Adverb phrases • Transformation of sentences with adverb phrases • Transformation of simple, complex and compound sentences	• Listening comprehension: fill in the blanks • Enacting a poem	• Descriptive account
18. Twelfth Night	New Beginnings	• Archaic words	• Direct and indirect speech	• Conversation: thanking for help • Intonation: stressing on different words in a sentence	• Writing a report • Making a poster
Assessment (SAFAL)					

Contents

1 Three Questions

Comprehension

Read this extract from 'Kabuliwallah', a famous story by Rabindranath Tagore, and answer the questions that follow.

My five-year-old daughter Mini cannot live without chattering. I really believe that in all her life she has not wasted a minute in silence. Her mother is often vexed at this, and would stop her prattle, but I would not. To see Mini quiet is unnatural, and I cannot bear it long. And so my own talk with her is always lively.

One morning, for instance, when I was in the midst of the seventeenth chapter of my new novel, my little Mini stole into the room, and putting her hand into mine, said: 'Father! Ramdayal the doorkeeper calls a crow a *krow*! He doesn't know anything, does he?'

Before I could explain to her the differences of language in this world, she had embarked on the full tide of another subject. 'What do you think, Father? Bhola says there is an elephant in the clouds, blowing water out of his trunk, and that is why it rains!'

And then, darting off anew, while I sat still making ready some reply to this last saying, 'Father! what relation is Mother to you?'

'My dear little sister in the law!' I murmured involuntarily to myself, but with a grave face contrived to answer: 'Go and play with Bhola, Mini! I am busy!'

The window of my room overlooks the road. The child had seated herself at my feet near my table, and was playing softly, drumming on her knees. I was hard at work on my seventeenth chapter, where Pratap Singh, the hero, had just caught Kanchanlata, the heroine, in his arms, and was about to escape with her by the third storey window of the castle, when all of a sudden Mini left her play, and ran to the window, crying, 'A Kabuliwallah! A Kabuliwallah!' Sure enough in the street below was a Kabuliwallah, passing slowly along. He wore the loose soiled clothing of his people, with a tall turban; there was a bag on his back, and he carried boxes of grapes in his hand.

I cannot tell what were my daughter's feelings at the sight of this man, but she began to call him loudly. 'Ah!' I thought, 'He will come in, and my seventeenth chapter will never be finished!' At which exact moment the Kabuliwallah turned, and looked up at the child. When she saw this, overcome by terror, she fled to her mother's protection, and disappeared. She had a blind belief that inside the bag, which the big man carried, there were perhaps two or three other children like herself. The peddler meanwhile entered my doorway, and greeted me with a smiling face.

So precarious was the position of my hero and my heroine that my first impulse was to stop and buy something, since the man had been called. I made some small purchases, and a conversation began about Abdurrahman, the Russians, the English and the Frontier Policy.

As he was about to leave, he asked: 'And where is the little girl, sir?'

And I, thinking that Mini must get rid of her false fear, had her brought out.

She stood by my chair, and looked at the Kabuliwallah and his bag. He offered her nuts and raisins, but she would not be tempted, and only clung closer to me, with all her doubts increased.

This was their first meeting.

1. Write the meanings of the following words as used in the extract.
   a. prattle: ____________
   b. unnatural: ____________
   c. embarked: ____________
   d. darting off: ____________
   e. precarious: ____________
2. What were the differing views of Mini's father and mother regarding her chattering?
3. What kind of a child was Mini?
4. What was Mini's father's profession? How do we know about it?
5. Describe the first encounter of Mini and the Kabuliwallah.
6. Why do you think Mini called out to him? Why was she frightened?
7. What was the most endearing moment in this extract for you?
8. '*...He doesn't know anything, does he?*'
   a. Who said this and to whom?
   b. Who is referred to as 'he' here?

c. What had 'he' said?

____

____

9. *'And where is the little girl, sir?'*

a. Who said this and to whom?

____

b. Why did the 'little girl' flee to her mother's protection?

____

____

c. Who brought the 'little girl' out? Why?

____

____

____

Way with Words

Forming Words Using Prefixes and Suffixes

A. Form new words by adding these prefixes and suffixes to the words within the brackets. Then complete the sentences using the newly formed words.

un-	mis-	-worthy	dis-	-able	over-

1. Opu's eyes widened in __________ (belief) as he read the book.
2. Opu decided to __________ (come) his initial hesitation and follow the instructions given in the book.
3. The __________ (behaviour) of the cowherd boy angered Opu's mother.
4. Opu strongly believed that his dream of flying was __________ (achieve).
5. Opu's efforts were __________ (praise).
6. Opu had __________ (knowingly) been tricked.

B. Do as directed.

1. Form opposites of these adjectives by using the prefix *dis-*.

content: ______________________

similar: ______________________

orderly: ______________________

2. Form opposites of these nouns by adding the prefix *mis-*.

fortune: ______________________

trust: ______________________

conduct: ______________________

3. **Form abstract nouns by adding the suffix *-tion* to these verbs.**

continue: ______________________

interact: ______________________

explain: ______________________

4. **Form adverbs by adding the suffix *-ly* to these adjectives.**

massive: ______________________

effortless: ______________________

partial: ______________________

5. **Form new words by adding the prefix *con-* to these words.**

cave: ______________________

sequence: ______________________

cord: ______________________

6. **Form new words by adding the suffix *-able* to the words.**

read: ______________________

recognise: ______________________

comfort: ______________________

Synonyms

C. Complete the following sentences using a synonym for the words or phrases in italics.

1. Rohit will *arrive* this evening but his family will only ________________ tonight in a later flight.
2. A loud *blast* was heard near the railway station and this was followed by another ________________.
3. This medicine will *ease* your headache and ________________ your stressed back.
4. If you are looking for a *quick way* to go to the airport, you need to ask a taxi driver; they know all the ________________.
5. The teacher instructed the students to *join* the two pieces of paper with glue and then ________________ it to the cardboard.

D. Rewrite the sentences using the synonyms of the italicised words. Use the clues given in the brackets.

1. The upper reaches of the Nile river are difficult to *navigate* without an experienced pilot. (transfer/steer/journey)

____

2. By the end of the play, the villain was filled with *remorse* and promised to make amends for all his actions. (regret/anger/fear)

____

3. The heat and continuous *exertion* on the field made her feel faint. (hard work/excitement/commotion)

____

4. A *conflict* can only be resolved through discussion and debate. (situation/disagreement/conversation)

____

5. The *ultimate* source of all energy is the sun. (final/basic/peak)

____

6. Many doctors advise *brisk* walk to burn off extra calories. (fast/slow/leisurely)

____

7. The nest of the bird rested on a *fragile* branch. (sturdy/delicate/broken)

____

8. There was a candlestick in every *niche* in that room. (recess/pillar/wall)

____

Grammar in Use

TRANSITIVE AND INTRANSITIVE VERBS

Read these sentences.

He **carried** boxes of grapes in his hand.

I **murmured** involuntarily.

In the first sentence, the verb **carried** needs the object 'boxes of grapes' to make complete sense.

A verb which requires an object to make complete sense is called a **transitive verb**. When a verb has two objects, one is a direct object, while the other is an indirect object.

In the second sentence, the verb **murmured** makes complete sense on its own.

A verb which does not require an object to make complete sense is called an **intransitive verb**. Such verbs can stand alone or may be followed by a phrase that gives information about the action.

A. Identify the italicised verbs in the sentences as transitive (T) or intransitive (I).

1. The little boy *danced* well. ________
2. I *showed* her my scrapbook. ________
3. She *giggled* at the suggestion. ________
4. I *ate* all the cookies. ________
5. He *keeps* his money in his wallet. ________
6. He *slept* on a bench that night. ________
7. I *play* chess with my father at night. ________

8. I *answered* the question loudly. __________

9. The train *leaves* at 10 p.m. sharp. __________

10. The coach *shouted* at the players for performing poorly. __________

USING FEW/A FEW, LITTLE/A LITTLE, LITTLE/LESS

B. You know that the words few, a few, little, a little, less and more all indicate quantity. Now, complete the sentences using the words in the box. Some of the words may be used more than once.

few	a few	little	a little	less	more

1. __________ blankets will not be enough for the countless refugees.
2. We have __________ to worry about now.
3. __________ people care to follow traffic rules sincerely.
4. Decisions based on __________ information can be dangerous.
5. She earns a lot __________ than I do, so she can afford certain luxuries.
6. Only __________ students managed to pass the difficult exam.
7. We had only __________ coins left for the games.
8. The audition generated __________ interest in the students. Many did not turn up for it.
9. __________ kindness goes a long way in helping others.

Listening and Speaking

Work in pairs to enact a conversation between two new friends who ask questions to find out more about each other's families. Use as many open-ended and close-ended questions as you can.

Pen it Down

You recently participated in a leadership training workshop in your school. Write an email to your friend telling him/her about your experience and learnings.

You can write about these points:

- the agenda and the duration of the training
- the trainer and his/her qualities
- the benefits that the training would bring to your life
- the most interesting part of the training

Selfhood

2 Hope is the Thing with Feathers

Way with Words

IMAGERY

Read these lines.

The moon was a ghostly galleon
tossed upon cloudy seas

These lines create a picture in our minds of the moon that is painted as a ghost ship upon clouds in the sky which resemble waves.

Now read the sentence.

The pungent smell of the spices filled the kitchen.

This sentence presents an image where we can almost smell the spices.

Imagery is the use of language such that it produces pictures in the readers' minds. It is not only visual but also paints images evoking senses of sound, touch, smell, taste and movement.

Complete the following sentences using the types of imagery given in brackets.

1. The dusty attic was filled with ______________________________. (visual)
2. The writer sat at his old typewriter and ______________________________. (touch)
3. When she took the cake out of the oven ______________________________. (smell)
4. The water from the well was ______________________________. (taste)
5. The song of the bird ______________________________. (sound)
6. The boat was rocking ______________________________. (visual)

Grammar in Use

Determiners

Determiners are words used before nouns to indicate which nouns are being referred to. They are either specific or general in meaning.

Examples: **This** decision to postpone the picnic was taken by all the students.
I have **a few** questions for you.

A. Complete the sentences with suitable determiners.

1. John and James are flying kites. ____________ (The/This) children are having fun.
2. Mummy gave me ____________ (an/a) blue sweater for ____________ (my/her) birthday.
3. ____________ (What/Which) house in this lane is yours?
4. ____________ (These/That) girl from our class can swim well.
5. We have ____________ (few/some) bread and cheese. So, we can make ____________ (our/my) favourite sandwich.
6. ____________ (Those/That) shoes on the rack are mine.
7. ____________ (My/Whose) parents are travelling to Europe ____________ (that/this) summer.
8. ____________ (Much/Most) students opted for extra English classes.

Phrases and Clauses

You know that a **phrase** is a group of words which conveys some meaning but does not make complete sense. It does not have a finite verb or a subject of its own.

However, a **clause** is a group of words that contains a subject and a finite verb. A clause can be a part of the sentence or a sentence by itself.

Examples: The girl **with the blue umbrella** is my sister. (phrase)
The girl **who is standing there** is my cousin. (clause)

B. Identify each underlined group of words as a phrase (P) or a clause (C).

1. The lady who is clapping is my mother. ______
2. The man with the beard is a criminal. ______
3. This is the place where the car ran out of fuel. ______
4. The peacock flew to our roof. ______
5. When I reached home, everyone had left. ______
6. Cycling uphill is a difficult task. ______
7. We woke up early to play football in the park. ______
8. The boy in the white shorts, who won the race, is receiving an award. ______

Listening and Speaking

A. Listen to the passage and answer the following questions.

1. What was the first question that the Caterpillar asked Alice?

2. Why did Alice hesitate to answer the first question?

3. What did the Caterpillar ask Alice to explain?

4. What would happen to the Caterpillar when he turned into a butterfly?

5. Why did Alice feel the Caterpillar would feel queer?

6. Why was Alice feeling irritated with this conversation?

7. Why did Alice decide to leave the Caterpillar?

8. Why did the Caterpillar want her to come back?

B. What, according to you, is the most important part of playing games? Is it to have fun or is it winning the game? Form two groups and have a debate on the topic 'Playing a game is fun only if you win it.'

You can use the following points:

For

- The main objective of a competition is to win it.
- Losing makes one sad.

Against

- Playing with friends is always fun.
- Winning and losing both make up the game. It is the spirit that matters.

Pen it Down

A. Imagine that you and your mother are going to visit an old-age home. You want your best friend to join you. Write a message to your friend informing him/her of the visit and requesting them to meet you at a designated place and time.

B. Imagine that your friend is upset as her final examinations are approaching and she feels that she has not prepared well yet. Write a paragraph on how being hopeful can help your friend. You can talk about the following points:

- how a positive outlook leads to confidence
- how one must not feel disappointed and should rather prepare a timetable to help with focus and motivation
- how one should seek their parents' and teachers' help in revising the lessons

3 Looking for Vultures' Eggs

Comprehension

Read this story and answer the questions that follow.

It was mid-January and a farmer was making his way back from the pond, a small fishing line dangling from his shoulders. A little freshwater shrimp and a couple of fish was all he had managed to catch that evening. As he made his way through the foggy darkness along the dirt road, he hummed an evergreen Bengali song to himself.

Suddenly, his pace slowed. He thought he heard a faint purr. He stopped. Yes, there it was again ... there must be a kitten somewhere. This man had an ardent love for all life forms and had fostered orphaned baby animals from his childhood. True to his old habits, he put his paraphernalia down and went looking for the kitten.

Slowly, he moved closer and closer to the source of the sound and then he saw it—a furry ball, a famished weakling. Instinctively, he picked it up, held it close to his chest and trudged back to his house. He had done this many a times before, fostered kittens and puppies. This meek thing was, thus, in the best hands—it would surely survive.

Golu, as the kitten came to be known, found a new mother in the farmer's wife. At first, he refused to eat or drink. The wife and the children stayed up and tried innumerable tricks to feed their newest family member, but to no avail, till the farmer dipped his index finger in milk and put it inside Golu's mouth. Instantly, Golu started sucking. His feeding problems were at last over. By and by, Golu started eating meat and seemed to get especially excited when fish was served.

Within six months, Golu had grown surprisingly large and was up to all kinds of impish antics. One evening, he casually strolled into a neighbour's yard and came upon his hen coop. As the chicken clucked in alarm, their owner came rushing out of the house, armed with a sturdy stick. Confronted by the enraged neighbour, Golu fluffed his body and bared his teeth. In the fading light of day, his shadow elongated by the man's lamp, he presented a monstrous vision that sent the neighbour screaming blue murder. Golu made a smart exit and nonchalantly assumed his usual pose on the porch of his house, the very picture of innocence.

Another day, he chased a little Black Bengal goat while its mother pitifully bleated her agony. However, this time he was seen by people in broad daylight. Golu had been caught red-handed. The neighbours decided to pay his owner a visit to ask him to contain this leopard cub or tiger cub or whatever it was ... because it certainly wasn't a house cat! But the moment they stepped inside the compound of the house, Golu expressed his disapproval. He arched his back, his fur stood on end and his teeth gleamed as he surveyed the intruders to his territory.

Not until his mother reprimanded him did Golu reluctantly settle down. He was like a Doberman, a one-master cat who had made it very clear to the neighbours that he neither liked them nor did he consider them fit to be listened to. As the laundry list of complaints against the cat grew, a verdict was passed. Strong iron chains were ordered for Golu and henceforth, he was to be tied and kept inside the boundaries of his house. The neighbours were content. They could sleep peacefully now; the hens could be let loose in the backyards and the goats could bleat and frolic without the fear of a mischievous cat prowling the vicinity.

– Tiasa Adhya

A. Answer these questions in your own words.

1. What made the farmer respond to the cry of the animal?

2. How did the farmer's family try to get Golu to feed?

3. Describe briefly any one incident from the passage that proved Golu was no ordinary cat.

4. How did the people try to find a solution to the problems caused by Golu?

5. What benefits did they expect from this solution?

6. How was the farmer's attitude towards Golu different from that of his neighbours?

B. Make sentences with these idioms from the story.

1. in safe hands

2. screaming blue murder

3. caught red handed

C. Write the synonyms of these words from the story. One is done for you.

1. ardent: *keen, eager*
2. meek: ____________________
3. trudge: ____________________
4. verdict: ____________________
5. nonchalant: ____________________
6. impish: ____________________

Way with Words

Collocations

A **collocation** is a combination of words in a language that occurs quite often and more frequently than would happen by chance.

Examples: strong coffee   resounding success

A. Match the words in Column A with the words they collocate with in Column B.

A	B
1. waste	a. the moment
2. seize	b. a tribute
3. pay	c. an opportunity
4. give	d. a good time
5. make	e. a compliment
6. have	f. a mistake

B. Use the collocations from the previous exercise in sentences of your own.

1. ____________________
2. ____________________
3. ____________________
4. ____________________
5. ____________________
6. ____________________

C. Choose the correct options to complete the collocations.

1. a (powerful/mighty) car
2. a leisurely (run/stroll)
3. an (undetectable/incurable) disease

4. a (firm/tough) handshake
5. a (routine/regular) check
6. a (rough/fierce) argument
7. to the (line/point) answer
8. immediate (family/relatives)

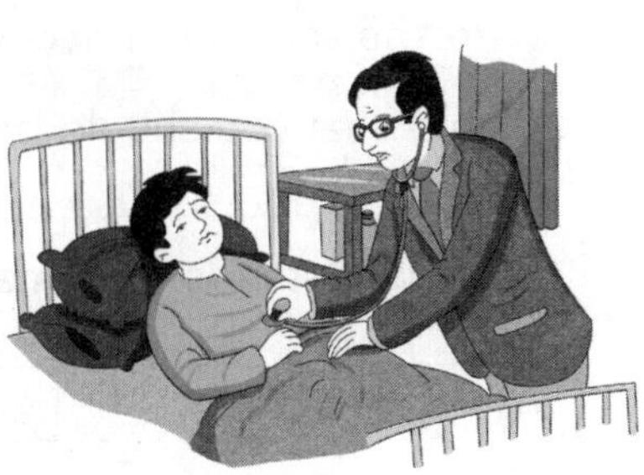

Word Association

D. Underline the odd word in each of the following set of words.

1. luxury	antique	original	traditional
2. demanding	challenging	tiring	rewarding
3. painting	news	advertising	films
4. artist	sculptor	engineer	actor
5. parody	caricature	skit	tragedy

Grammar in Use

Converting Adjectives to Nouns

You know that adjectives can be converted into nouns by adding different suffixes.

Examples: happy – happiness, possible – possibility

A. Complete the sentences using the noun forms of the italicised adjectives.

1. The *loyal* son was blessed by his father and his __________ was rewarded when the father gifted him a watch on his birthday.
2. The Commanding Officer of the army was extremely *angry* to see his order disobeyed, but his __________ soon melted away when he realised that the soldiers were truly repentant.
3. It takes a *wise* man to forgive other's mistakes, but it takes even more __________ to admit one's own mistakes.
4. The sudden __________ in the *weak* woman's legs made her stumble.
5. Mohita has always been very *independent* – having a car has improved her __________.

Transformation of Sentences

You have learnt that each of the four types of sentences, namely assertive, interrogative, exclamatory and interrogative, can be changed to the other types.

Examples: Do you know where Ramya lives? (interrogative)
I don't know where Ramya lives. (assertive)

B. Rewrite the sentences according to the instructions.

1. Is this what you should be wearing to the wedding? (Change to an assertive sentence.)

   ____

2. She understands what makes me so upset. (Change to an interrogative sentence.)

   ____

3. Will their bravery ever be forgotten? (Change to an assertive sentence.)

   ____

4. I can never remember the phone numbers of my friends. (Change to an interrogative sentence.)

   ____

5. Who does not love a large bowl of ice cream on a hot day? (Change to an assertive sentence.)

   ____

6. Everyone was eagerly waiting for the results to be declared. (Change to an interrogative sentence.)

   ____

7. Can the match be played in this weather? (Change to an assertive sentence.)

   ____

8. One cannot help admire the cleverness of Sherlock Holmes. (Change to an interrogative sentence.)

   ____

9. Has he directed any good film in the recent past? (Change to an assertive sentence.)

   ____

10. This is the kind of story I like to read. (Change to an interrogative sentence.)

   ____

Listening and Speaking

A. Work in groups of three. Imagine that you have visited an Indian hill station. You are sightseeing and having fun. Describe what you see. Ask your group members to identify the place. Take turns to describe and guess different hill stations.

B. Is there any place that you dream of visiting one day? Tell your class about your dream holiday destination and what you would like to do there.

You may include the following details:

- the tourist attractions related to the destination
- why you want to visit it
- who do you want to visit it with

Pen it Down

A. Reading storybooks can transport us to an imaginative world full of adventures. However, some children do not like reading storybooks and would rather spend their time playing games. Do you think reading storybooks should be made compulsory for everyone? Write your views either for or against this topic.

B. Read the given beginning of a story. In about 200 words, write an alternate ending to the story.

The pilot announced that the aircraft was about to make its descent. Sonia looked out of the window and watched the houses look larger and larger. This was the first time she was flying with her family. Her parents and little sister were sitting a few seats away. As the plane landed, she turned around and waved to them, saying that she would meet them at the exit. She got off the plane and waited at the exit for them to join her. Soon the plane was empty, and to her dismay she could not find her family. They had disappeared!...

4 Coromandel Fishers

Way with Words

Idioms

Read this sentence.

If you criticise Mohit, it's like a red rag to a bull—he gets absolutely furious.

Here, the underlined phrase is an idiom.

An **idiom** is a group of words whose meaning is different from the meanings of the individual words.

Complete the sentences using the idioms from the box below.

back to square one	eleventh hour	have second thoughts
let the cat out of the bag	nineteen to the dozen	on cloud nine
costs an arm and a leg	a method to his madness	cut corners

1. Gina's youngest daughter talks ________________ and is the centre of attention at any party.
2. At the ________________ they managed to arrange enough money to buy the house.
3. Sarah was ________________ the day her results were declared as she had managed to secure the first position in class.
4. Nobody would have known their secret. We only got to know because Nishant ________________.
5. After all the effort, Vikram found himself ________________ when the doctor pronounced him unfit to play.
6. The overcoat I want to buy ________________.
7. Sneha was starting to ________________ about the vacation when she heard the weather alerts.
8. Though the detective seems to be eccentric, there is ________________.
9. The company has ________________ to make its new phone powerful yet affordable.

Grammar in Use

Assertive and Exclamatory Sentences

We can interchange assertive and exclamatory sentences, without changing their meanings.

Examples: 1. What a delicious meal! (exclamatory)
It is a delicious meal. (assertive)

2. Our team played brilliantly. (assertive)
How brilliantly our team played! (exclamatory)

Rewrite the following sentences according to the instructions without changing their meaning.

1. What an exciting match! (Change to an assertive sentence.)
____
2. It was a very tiring day for the diggers. (Change to an exclamatory sentence.)
____
3. Alas! The team could not make it to the finals. (Begin: It was ...)
____
4. How nice of you to remember my birthday! (Begin: It ...)
____
5. I wish I could travel forever. (Change to an exclamatory sentence.)
____
6. It is quite hot today. (Begin: How hot ...)
____
7. The project is very confusing. (Change to an exclamatory sentence.)
____

Listening and Speaking

Listen to the first two stanzas of the poem 'The Solitary Reaper' by William Wordsworth. Recite them with the correct intonation.

Behold her, single in the field,
Yon solitary Highland Lass!
Reaping and singing by herself;
Stop here, or gently pass!
Alone she cuts and binds the grain,
And sings a melancholy strain;
O listen! for the Vale profound
Is overflowing with the sound.

No Nightingale did ever chaunt
More welcome notes to weary bands
Of travellers in some shady haunt,
Among Arabian sands:
A voice so thrilling ne'er was heard
In spring-time from the Cuckoo-bird,
Breaking the silence of the seas
Among the farthest Hebrides.

Pen it Down

Write an essay on what profession you would like to pursue in your life. It need not be the careers usually opted for. Give reasons for your choice.

5 Where Tigers Swim

Comprehension

Read this passage and answer the questions that follow.

An ancient nation like India is an incredible repository of heritage in various forms– culture, architecture, music, performing arts, refined arts, textiles and so much more.

The Indian National Trust for Art and Cultural Heritage or INTACH was established in 1984 in New Delhi, with a single minded purpose to spread awareness about the conservation of heritage in India. It soon opened up different branches or chapters in different parts of the country with the passage of time, with the aim to promote, preserve and propagate the cause of heritage in regional and local contexts. There are 190 chapters at present making it one of the world's largest heritage organisations.

Exploring oral histories is one of their areas of interest as history is not limited to the exploits of kings, queens and conquerors. It is also the story of ordinary people. For this purpose it has collaborated with the Centre for Community Knowledge (CCK) of Ambedkar University to organise a month-long event in Mehrauli in a bid to showcase the narratives of the people of Delhi and their lifestyle. INTACH Delhi chapter convenor Swapna Liddle remarked, 'This kind of initiative encourages the community to participate in restoring oral and cultural heritage and ultimately preserves the area.'

The presentation is in the form a 'neighbourhood museum' or a 'pop-up museum' highlighting the lost or almost lost stories of the people of Delhi from days of yore. This is the third edition of the 'Neighbourhood Museum' series. The first one was held in Shadi Khampur, a Jat majority village, in 2012, followed by another one in Nizamuddin in 2015. Surajit Sarkar, associate professor and coordinator at CCK, said that the idea behind the initiative is to unearth stories of common man relevant to life within a community.

According to the collaborators, the venue of the event can be in any premises in the colony like a *haveli* or a locality park. People from the city are interviewed for their stories, and then photographs and artefacts are documented and exhibited at the venue. The university ties up with a social organisation, community group, or an institution for an insightful perspective.

Events that will form a part of the programme include exhibitions, discussions, workshops, and cultural events in which local citizens participate and share their folklore, songs, customs, and stories, which have been passed down from one generation to the next in the oral tradition. It would be a revisiting of existing cultural knowledge by engaging communities and representing the diversity of lives and livelihood of the city through dialogues, photographs, or artefacts. It also presents the fascinating growth of a neighbourhood of Delhi, according to Sarkar.

The plethora of information gathered through this concept will be archived in digital form and made available online after compilation.

Complimenting this endeavour made by the university, Liddle said the steps being taken by the university may pave the way for a city museum.

'Community or city museum is a common feature in foreign cities, but unfortunately Delhi has none. We have several museums and galleries in the city but there is no specific place where one can go and find information about the city and its people,' she said.

A. Answer the following questions.

1. What are the full forms of CCK and INTACH?

____

____

____

2. What are the 'Neighbourhood Museum' series?

____

____

____

3. What are the possible venues of the neighbourhood event?

____

____

____

4. Which events are being organised as part of the programme?

____

____

____

5. What is the role of a community or city museum?

____

____

____

B. Answer these questions with reference to context.

1. *'This kind of initiative encourages the community to participate in restoring oral and cultural heritage and ultimately preserves the area.'*

   a. Who said these words?

   ____

   ____

   b. What is the initiative that is being spoken of?

   ____

   ____

   ____

c. What is the advantage of such an initiative?

____

____

____

____

2. *It would be a revisiting of existing cultural knowledge by engaging communities...*

a. What events would form a part of this 'revisiting'?

____

____

____

____

____

____

b. How will the information be gathered?

____

____

c. How will this information be made available to all?

____

____

____

____

C. Read the given meanings. Fill in the blanks with the correct words from the box.

plethora	archive	convenor	repository
document	heritage	perspective	folklore

1. record something in written, photographic, or other form: ______________
2. inherited traditions, monuments, objects, and culture: ______________
3. a large or excessive amount of something: ______________
4. a person whose job is to call people together for meetings of a committee: ______________
5. store old records or documents so that one can access them again in the future: ______________
6. a point of view: ______________
7. stories of the ordinary people: ______________
8. storehouse: ______________

Way with Words

Compound Adjectives

Read this sentence.

Mohini's **three-year-old** daughter is very naughty.

Here, the words in bold is a compound adjective.

An adjective made up of two or more words with a hyphen between them is called a **compound adjective**.

A. Match the statements with the most appropriate compound adjectives. One is done for you.

high-spirited   well-behaved   self-confident   absent-minded
easy-going   self-reliant   self-conscious

1. I am not easily annoyed, worried or upset with things. *easy-going*
2. I always do well in school, and I know I will be successful. ________________
3. I am a practical joker and very popular with my classmates. ________________
4. I am never able to remember to return my library books on time. ________________
5. I can do things and take decisions by myself, without needing help from others. ________________
6. I love singing but I am too shy to participate in my school concerts. ________________
7. My teachers always compliment me on my good behaviour and conduct. ________________

Commonly Confused Words

B. Circle the correct options to complete these sentences. You may use a dictionary to look up the meanings of certain words.

1. If you require new stationary/stationery, there is a shop just around the corner.
2. He waited for the signal/sign to change and then started his car.
3. He is trying to evade/avoid the football coach as he has been missing out on regular practice/practise.
4. He seemed quite disinterested/uninterested in the discussion that was taking place.
5. He has a distinct flare/flair for business and will surely succeed in his new enterprise.

Grammar in Use

Types of Adjectives

A. Choose the correct options to complete the sentences.

1. Are girls ________ talkative than boys?
   a. most   b. more
2. Our team scored the ____________ points in the inter-school quiz contest.
   a. most   b. more
3. Kolkata is a ________ city.
   a. best   b. large
4. If you practise regularly, you will develop ___________ batting techniques.
   a. good   b. better
5. There was ________ milk in the bowl.
   a. much   b. no
6. I think he needs _______________ help with the project.
   a. least   b. a little
7. Please step forward ________ paces to the starting line.
   a. five   b. long
8. Have you read ________ of these books?
   a. all   b. many
9. ________ friends I have are very close to me.
   a. The few   b. A few
10. I have been to England ________ times.
    a. some   b. many

B. Read the sentences and identify the types of adjectives the underlined words are.

1. Which place do you belong to? ____________________
2. This bag is big enough to carry all the vegetables.
   ____
3. Delhi is a large city with a rich history. ____________________
4. The interviewers were looking for an honest candidate.
   ____
5. Only five out of twenty applicants were chosen.
   ____

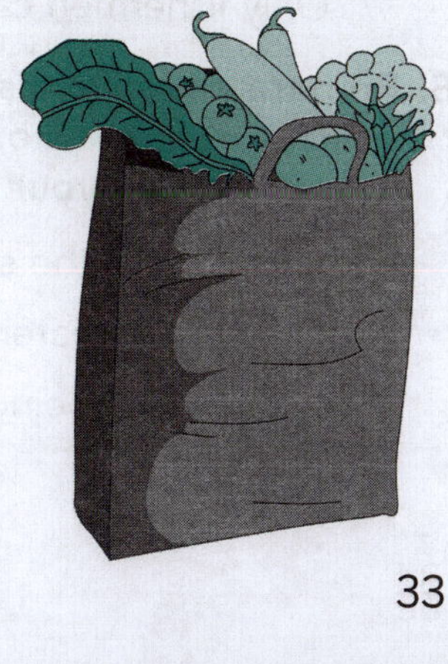

6. Which batsman scored a century today, Kohli or Dhoni? ____________

7. She is playing with her two young dogs. ____________

8. Many people were present at the gathering. ____________

9. I would like to decorate the venue with those flowers. ____________

10. Which colour suits you best? ____________

TENSES

> You have learnt that tenses are classified into the present, past and future tenses, which exist in the simple, continuous, perfect and perfect continuous forms.

C. Complete the sentences with the correct form of the tenses as given in brackets.

1. She ____________ (return) from the market when she ____________ (witness) the accident.
2. By 2022, India's population ____________ (overtake) that of China's.
3. When ____________ (do) one apply for a visa?
4. She ____________ (already finish) singing when I ____________ (announce) the next artist.
5. The sun ____________ (rise) in the east.
6. We ____________ (play) for an hour when the rain started.

Listening and Speaking

A. Listen to a passage about sea turtles and state whether these statements are true (T) or false (F). Correct the false statements.

1. There are more than five species of sea turtles. ☐
2. Sea turtles spend most of their life on beaches and coastal areas. ☐
3. Bycatch is the deliberate hunting of sea turtles. ☐
4. Only a few species of sea turtles are now classified as endangered. ☐
5. Sea turtles are sensitive to the magnetic field of the earth. ☐
6. Only female sea turtles remember the area they were born. ☐
7. Only fishermen can help in the conservation of sea turtles. ☐

B. Prepare and give a short presentation on an endangered species of animals of your choice. You may include these points in your presentation:

- the habitat of the species
- the factors threatening its survival
- the measures being taken for its conservation

Pen it Down

We all have a responsibility in contributing positively towards environmental issues. However, many people are aloof to the threats that loom over our environment and how these could affect us. Do you think it's only the responsibility of the government to enforce measures to protect the environment? Write an essay on your views either for or against this topic.

6

Composed upon Westminster Bridge, September 3, 1802

Comprehension

Read the passage carefully and answer the questions that follow.

'Are you sure that's a synagogue?' Israeli tourist Or Tovi sounded sceptical as we crossed the road. 'It has a clock tower; I think it's a church. I have never seen a synagogue which looks like this.' But once he set foot inside, his scepticism changed to open-mouthed awe. 'I have never seen a synagogue so beautiful. There is nothing like this in Israel.' Such is the magic of Kolkata's Maghen David, the grandest synagogue in the East.

Now, while most books or websites will tell you that Kolkata had two or perhaps three synagogues, it in fact had five, of which three survive. The first of these was the Neveh Shalom, dating back to 1831, and rebuilt in 1911. Next came Beth El in 1856. This was followed by the Maghen David in 1884, the Beth Ha Knesset on Blackburn Lane in 1897 (which later became the Maghen Aboth) and finally the Sha'are Rason in 1933.

Built on a grand scale in 1884 at the sole expense of Elias David Joseph Ezra, Maghen David took the place of the old Neveh Shalom. Externally, it is in the Kolkata Renaissance style. The clock tower is 42 metres high and the clock used to chime with five peals every quarter hour. But it is the interior that stuns visitors. The floor has black and white checkered tiles in some places and colourful mosaic in others. There is a large stained glass rose window right above the door. In the centre of the hall is the pulpit, where the Rabbi would be present. At one end of the hall, is a raised platform, with a half dome and three curtained doors. Behind the doors are Torah scrolls, holy artefacts; they are not for public display. The Beth El and the Maghen David at one point had a fine collection of Torah scrolls, but as the community left the city, the scrolls travelled with them, mostly to Israel.

The half dome referred to earlier is dark blue in colour and has golden stars painted on it, perhaps to imitate the heavens. Wooden stairs on the left and right of the door lead visitors up to a gallery, with seating arrangements for the ladies of the congregation. Originally lit by gas, the synagogue now has electric lights, and a most excellent set of chandeliers. As you walk around, if you are observant, you will find that much of the glass used in the lampshades comes from Belgium.

Few people are aware that the Maghen David narrowly escaped demolition during the construction of the Howrah Bridge. Now under the protection of the Archaeological Survey of India as a monument of national importance, Maghen David is very well maintained.

A. Answer the following questions.

1. Which synagogue is being spoken of here? How old is it?

2. Name the five synagogues of Kolkata.

3. What are Torah scrolls? What happened to the collection of scrolls at Maghen David?

4. Architecturally, which style does the synagogue follow?

5. In not more 60 words, describe the interiors of the Maghen David Synagogue.

6. What nearly happened to Maghen David years ago? Who maintains the synagogue now?

B. Complete the following sentences with words from the passage.

1. I am ____________ about our team's chances of winning the tournament.
2. The children stared ____________ at the screen.
3. The wedding was a very ____________ occasion.
4. Dolphins learn to ____________ sounds very accurately and quickly.
5. ____________ walkers may see red deer along this stretch of the road.

Way with Words

SIMILE

Read these lines.

I wandered lonely **as a cloud** that floats on high o'er vales and hills.

These lines contain the simile **lonely as a cloud**. The poet, wandering by himself, compares his loneliness to that of a cloud floating over hills and valleys.

A **simile** is a figure of speech that compares two different things with the help of the words 'like' or 'as'.

A. Underline the similes in these sentences. Then, state what each simile is comparing.

1. Her laughter was as melodious as the chiming of bells.

   ____

2. I am as hungry as a lion.

   ____

3. She glanced furtively like a frightened mouse.

   ____

4. They fought over the property like vultures.

   ____

5. I was as cool as a cucumber during the exam.

   ____

6. The detective was as sly as a fox.

   ____

Personification

Read this line.

The wind howled mournfully outside our tents.

In this sentence, the wind is described as if it were a person, using the verb 'howling' for it.

Personification is when we speak or write about a thing, an animal or an idea as if it has human qualities.

B. Match the nouns in column A with the human qualities associated with them in column B. Then use any four of them in sentences of your own.

A	B
1. storm	a. kind and benevolent
2. rain	b. cheeky and insolent
3. wind	c. all-seeing and silent
4. fire	d. galloping and hungry
5. sky	e. lurking stalker
6. panther	f. raging and thundering

____

____

____

____

C. Underline the personifications in the following lines. Then, explain them in your own words.

1. And that Autumn's on her way.

____

2. 'Ah, William, we're weary of weather,' said the sunflowers, shining with dew.

____

3. When all at once I saw a crowd, / A host, of golden daffodils; / Beside the lake, beneath the trees, / Fluttering and dancing in the breeze.

____

4. Fate had her imagination about her,

____

5. Earth felt the wound;

____

6. She sweeps with many-coloured brooms, / And leaves the shreds behind; / Oh, housewife in the evening west, / Come back, and dust the pond!

____

Grammar in Use

Perfect and Perfect Continuous Tense

You have learnt that the **perfect tenses** refer to an action that has already been completed. They take the following forms:

	Perfect	Perfect Continuous
Present	have completed	have been completing
Past	had completed	had been completing
Future	will have completed	will have been completing

Examples: I **have** never **seen** a synagogue which looks like this. (present perfect)

The synagogue **had** narrowly **escaped** demolition during the construction of the Howrah Bridge. (past perfect)

A. Fill in the blanks with the suitable forms of perfect and perfect continuous tenses.

1. The children ________________ (practise) for the choir yesterday.
2. The train ________________ (leave) the station already.
3. The boys ________________ (learn) the alphabet for a month now.
4. The flowers ________________ (dance) in the breeze all day.
5. They ________________ (send) the notice to the parents by next week.
6. We ________________ (anticipate) the end of the crisis for a while now.

Punctuation

B. Rewrite the passage using correct punctuation marks.

soon a servant came from the house and told phatik his mother wanted him? phatik refused to move; but the servant was the master on this occasion! he took phatik up roughly and carried him! While he was kicking and struggling in rage-

when phatik came into the house (his mother said angrily) so you have been hitting makhan again.

phatik answered indignantly: 'No, I haven't? who told you that.'

his mother shouted? don't tell lies? you have?

phatik said suddenly i tell you lies, I haven't? You ask makhan but makhan thought it best to stick to his previous statement? he said yes mother? phatik did hit me

____

____

____

____

____

____

Apostrophe

C. Rewrite the sentences inserting apostrophe where necessary.

1. Lets go to the sports complex today.
2. Theyve been playing all afternoon.
3. Its time they came back home for dinner.
4. I wont be able to stay for lunch.
5. Rimas mother brought her a lot of books from the library.
6. You shouldnt run on wet ground. Youll fall.
7. The weathers beautiful today. Lets go for a stroll.
8. Rahuls family belongs to a small village in Gujarat.

Listening and Speaking

A. Imagine a situation where you have gone to your friend's house for lunch. You accidentally come across a notebook in their room titled 'My Little Book of Verses'. You read some pages of it and conclude that your friend is a great poet. Work in pairs and enact a conversation expressing your admiration for your friend's poems.

You may talk about these points:

- what the notebook consists of
- how the themes of the poems change from page to page
- how it inspires you

B. Read these lines from the poem 'The Land of Story Books' by R. L. Stevenson. Then, divide the words into syllables and underline the stressed syllables.

At evening when the lamp is lit,
Around the fire my parents sit;
They sit at home and talk and sing,
And do not play at anything.

Pen it Down

A. Imagine that your city is hosting an important sporting event and you are very excited about it. Write an email to a friend, inviting him/her to visit you during the event. Mention the sports the events will cover, along with their planned dates and time.

B. Look at this image of a beautiful park in your neighbourhood. Write a paragraph describing one of your visits to the park. Also compare it with the busy streets of your neighbourhood.

7 Mary Shelley

Comprehension

Read this extract from the novel 'Frankenstein' by Mary Shelley and answer the questions that follow.

For several months afterward, I stayed in bed, suffering from a nervous fever. Then, a letter from my father arrived, telling me that my youngest brother William had been found murdered. I knew I had to return home immediately.

It was completely dark when I arrived in Geneva. The gates of the town were shut, and I was forced to pass the night at a village outside. A storm was raging in the mountains. I wandered out to watch it, and with little concern for my safety, decided to visit the spot where poor William had been murdered.

Suddenly, in the darkness, I saw a figure lurking behind a clump of trees near me. A flash of lightning lit up the sky, and revealed the gigantic and deformed shape of the creature. It was the wretch whom I had brought to life. What was he doing here? Could he be the murderer of my brother?

I was convinced of it the moment the thought entered my mind. The creature passed me quickly, and I lost him in the gloom. I thought of following him, but another flash showed him hanging among the rocks. With unnatural speed, he soon reached the summit of the mountain and disappeared.

I entered my father's house at five in the morning. It was a house in mourning, and from that time I lived in daily fear of the monster's wickedness.

One day I had wandered off alone up the valley of Chamonix, and was resting along the side of the mountain, when I saw a man coming towards me over the crevices in the ice at superhuman speed. It was the monster, and his face was filled with bitter anguish.

'Begone!' I exclaimed 'Or, rather, stay, that I may turn you to dust!'

'I expected this reception,' said the monster. 'All men hate the wretched! I must be the most hated of them all. But if you agree to my conditions, I will leave the world of men and you at peace. If you refuse, be prepared for the death of your remaining loved ones.'

I was furious, but he continued: 'Have I not suffered enough? Remember that I am your creature. All around me, I see happiness, but I am excluded from it. I was compassionate, but misery made me a demon. I have helped people, I have saved people's lives when they were in danger, but I have been stoned and shot at in return. The desert mountains and colourless glaciers are now my refuge. Only the bleak sky is kind to me. Listen to me, Frankenstein, I am alone and miserable, and only one who is just like myself would be my loyal companion. You must create a woman for me who will be my bride.'

'Our lives might not be happy, but they will be harmless. You shall never see us again: We will go away to the vast wilds of South America, and my life will flow quietly away.'

I pitied him, then, and replied: 'I agree to your demand, but only on your solemn promise to leave Europe forever.'

'I swear,' he cried, 'Go home, and start working: I shall watch the progress with anxiety.'

I left for England with my friend Henry Clerval. I continued on to the remotest part of the Orkney Islands, where I would work to create a bride for the creature.

Three years ago, I had created a fiend and was now about to create another. I did not know what kind of a person she would be. Even if they were to leave Europe, their children might terrorize mankind.

I was alone on a solitary island, when the monster that I dreaded, appeared. By then, my mind was made up: I would never create another like him.

'Begone!' I cried, 'I break my promise. I will never create a being that might be like you in wickedness.'

The monster gnashed his teeth in anger. 'Will every man find a wife for himself, and I be alone? I had feelings of affection, and they were returned by hatred and scorn. I am leaving now, as you ask, but remember, I will always be with you.'

I rushed forward to stop him, but he left the house at great speed after delivering his terrible threat.

The next day I set off to rejoin Clerval and return home. But I never saw my friend again. The monster had taken his life too, as I found out soon.

A. State whether the following sentences are true (T) or false (F).

1. The narrator's brother had been murdered in Geneva. ☐
2. The narrator met the monstrous creature in the valley of Chamonix. ☐
3. The monster threatened to kill himself as all men hated him. ☐
4. The monster blamed the narrator for his misfortunes. ☐
5. The narrator created a bride for the monster in order to save the rest of his family from certain death. ☐
6. The monster promised never to meet his creator again. ☐

B. Answer the following questions with reference to context.

1. *'Begone!' I exclaimed 'Or, rather, stay, that I may turn you to dust!'*
   a. Who said these words and to whom?

   ____

   b. Why was the speaker angry at this person?

   ____

   ____

   ____

   c. What did the listener threaten to do? Where did he find comfort?

   ____

   ____

   ____

2. *'Begone!' I cried, 'I break my promise.'*

a. Where was the speaker at the time of this conversation?

b. What promise had the speaker made? Why did he intend to break that promise?

c. With what great threat did the listener leave the speaker?

d. Who was the listener's final victim?

C. The passage describes the hateful relationship between the narrator and the creature he gave life to. Match the following words describing intense negative feelings with their meanings.

Word	Meaning
1. hostility	a. disgust
2. revulsion	b. loathing
3. scorn	c. enmity
4. abhorrence	d. disrespect
5. aversion	e. unwillingness

Way with Words

Word Meanings

A. Look at the words given in the box. Match them with their meanings. You may use a dictionary.

serenity	languor	apprehension	exhilaration	inhibition
astonishment	perplexity	magnanimity	contentment	sympathy

1. ____________ is a feeling of self-consciousness or insecurity.
2. ____________ is a feeling of listlessness or apathy.
3. ____________ is a feeling of great excitement.

4. ________________ is a feeling of peacefulness.
5. ________________ is a feeling of satisfaction.
6. ________________ is a feeling of distress.
7. ________________ is a feeling of bewilderment.
8. ________________ is a feeling of generosity.
9. ________________ is a feeling of surprise.
10. ________________ is a feeling of pity for others.

FORMING ANTONYMS WITH PREFIXES

You know that we can form antonyms using prefixes.

Examples: important – **un**important
like – **dis**like
reversible- **ir**reversible

B. Complete the following sentences with the antonyms of the words in brackets. Remember to form the antonyms by adding suitable prefixes to the words.

1. One must not __________ (regard) the advice of elders.
2. It is an __________ (significant) mistake, do not be fussy about it.
3. __________ (invited) guests are not allowed in the premises.
4. We have to __________ (arrange) the flowers as per the instructions of the decorator.
5. It is very common to __________ (spell) words with silent alphabets.
6. The organization must be __________ (partial) in its dealings.

Grammar in Use

ADJECTIVE AND NOUN PHRASES

You have learnt about the different types of phrases.

An **adjective phrase** modifies the noun in a sentence.

Example: His face was filled **with bitter anguish**.

A **noun phrase** does the work of a noun, and acts as the subject or object in a sentence. It answers the questions *what* and *who*.

Example: **The gates of the town** were shut.

A. Identify each underlined sets of words as a noun phrase (NP) or an adjective phrase (AP).

1. I love exploring new places. ______
2. I know my tables till twenty. ______
3. Shree lost his dark brown suitcase at the airport. ______

4. I met my cousin sisters yesterday. ________
5. We were looking for clean and comfortable rooms. ________
6. Sivanshu bought very expensive shoes. ________
7. I don't have a bank account yet. ________
8. I took medicines for the chronic dry cough. ________
9. We ate some delicious food last night. ________

TRANSFORMATION OF SENTENCES WITH ADJECTIVE PHRASES

Read the following sentences.

We visited a **deserted** village.

We visited a village **without inhabitants**.

Both the sentences mean the same. In the second sentence, the adjective **deserted** is replaced with the adjective phrase **without inhabitants**. This is how we can transform sentences with adjective phrases.

B. Replace the adjectives in the following sentences with adjective phrases, without changing the meaning.

1. Hitesh wore a golden crown.

____

2. Rajni is a promising talent.

____

3. Caged beasts are a horrible sight.

____

4. Mr Khanna is an honourable man.

____

5. This is a courageous deed and must be rewarded.

____

6. Mimi was wearing a yellow hat.

____

Listening and Speaking

Have you ever had a day, which you would like to erase from your memory? Talk about it in class, in brief.

You can use the following points:

- what happened on the day
- how did it make you feel then
- how does it make you feel now

Pen it Down

Imagine that your school has recently formed a drama club and appointed you as its secretary. Write a notice inviting students from classes 6–8 to the first meeting of the club, to plan and discuss the different events that the club could organise. Mention the details of the meeting along with the date and time.

Family

8
Grannie

Way with Words

Emotive Language

Read this sentence.

Tears streamed down the mud-splattered face of the boy, who stood in tatters, holding out an empty bowl before the man.

Here, the details about the description of the boy create a feeling of pity for him. This is an example of how emotive language can be used to create sympathy for a character.

Emotive language is used to evoke a specific emotional response from the readers.

A. Rewrite the following sentences using emotive language. You may use up to two sentences each to create an emotional effect.

1. There was no transport available for ordinary workers.

2. The only earning member of the family had passed away.

3. The fields were filled with ripe corn.

4. The football match was won in the penalty shootout.

5. The storm caused a lot of damage to the village.

6. The stand-up comedian was applauded for his act.

____

____

Phrasal Verbs

Read this sentence.

Passers-by simply **looked on** as the two rival gangs started fighting.

In this sentence, the words in bold are an example of a phrasal verb. **Looked on** means 'to watch something without becoming involved in it yourself'.

A **phrasal verb** is a verb combined with an adverb or a preposition, or sometimes both, which has a particular meaning.

B. Complete the sentences using phrasal verbs with stand and back. Choose words from the box to form the phrasal verbs. You may need to change the forms of some of the verbs.

pull	in	by	date	get	sit	hold	away	up	aside

1. 'Stand __________ from the railing,' shouted the security guard.
2. After heading the party for twenty years, the chief decided it was time to stand __________ for the public.
3. The researcher found a marble statue __________ back to the 1800s.
4. A junior actor would now stand __________ for the popular actor.
5. After the nightmare, I just couldn't __________ back to sleep.
6. The crowd stood __________ and watched the man being harassed by the goons.
7. Police __________ the crowd back from the main road.
8. The emergency buses were kept on a stand __________.
9. At the theatre, we decided to just __________ back and enjoy the film.
10. The general decided to __________ back the troops from the post.

Grammar in Use

Question Tags

Read the given sentences.

Jai is coming to the party, **isn't he**?

You haven't read the book, **have you**?

In these sentences, the groups of words in bold are **question tags**.

A **question tag** is a phrase that is added to the end of a statement in order to turn it into a question or check that the statement is correct.

A. Complete the sentences using suitable question tags.

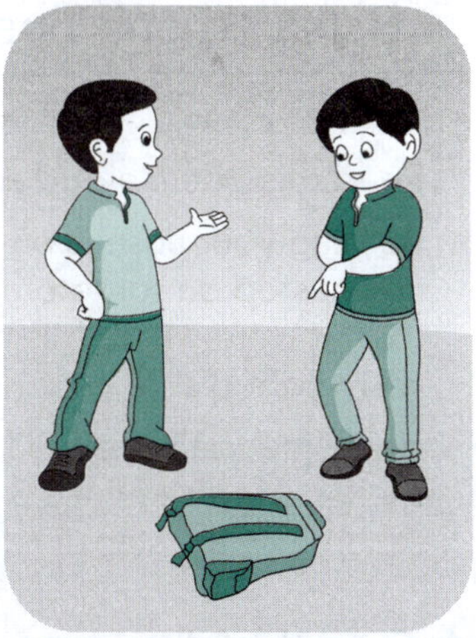

1. You are his friend, ______________?
2. They won't return to their villages, ______________?
3. This is not his bag, ______________?
4. She ate your fruits, ______________?
5. There is no way to predict the future, ______________?
6. We are going to win this match, ______________?
7. He won't do it again, ______________?
8. It hasn't rained since morning, ______________?
9. Let's have a cup of coffee, ______________?
10. We haven't met our new neighbours, ______________?

COMPARISON OF ADJECTIVES

You know that adjectives have three degrees of comparison: positive, comparative and superlative.

When we compare a particular quality of two things or persons, we add **-er** or **more** to the adjective. This is the comparative form.

When we compare a particular quality of more than two things or persons, we add **-est** or **most** to the adjective. This is the superlative form.

Examples: hard – harder – hardest
beautiful – more beautiful – most beautiful

B. Rewrite the following sentences according to the given starting words.

1. Delhi is one of the most polluted cities of the country.
   Very few ______________.
2. Sheena is the fastest bowler in the team.
   No other ______________.
3. Kalidasa was the most famous playwright of the Gupta Age.
   No other ______________.
4. India is one of the most active members of the United Nations.
   Few other ______________.
5. Aryan is the cleverest boy in the class.
   No other ______________.
6. Very few people are as enthusiastic about the project as he is.
   He is ______________.
7. Few other states in India use forests in an environmentally sustainable way as Sikkim does.
   Sikkim uses ______________.

Listening and Speaking

Read this poem aloud and note the rhyme scheme.

Be glad your nose is on your face,
not pasted on some other place,
for if it were where it is not,
you might dislike your nose a lot.

Here, the last words of lines 1 and 2 rhyme and hence may be given the name 'a'; similarly, the last words of lines 3 and 4 rhyme and hence may be given the name 'b'. Thus, the rhyme scheme of the stanza is *aabb*.

A. Read the following stanza and identify the rhyme scheme.

'Twas brillig, and the slithy toves
    Did gyre and gimble in the wabe:
All mimsy were the borogoves,
    And the mome raths outgrabe.
'Beware the Jabberwock, my son!
    The jaws that bite, the claws that catch!
Beware the Jubjub bird, and shun
    The frumious Bandersnatch!' ________________

B. Most families usually think about getting a pet. Children are especially enthusiastic about this, and the pet becomes an important family member. However, there are many families that cannot afford to keep a pet or have other problems that stop them from adopting a pet. Work in two groups and have a debate in class on the topic 'A family is incomplete without a pet.'

You can use the following points:

For

- A pet helps develop non-verbal communication, compassion and empathy.
- A pet brings joy to a family.

Against

- Pets might bring added set of responsibilities with it.
- Pets do not have long life spans and the loss of a pet might lead to unwanted trauma.

Pen it Down

Your school is celebrating Grandparents' Day. Design a poster announcing the events scheduled for the day, along with the date, time and venue. You may also include a line or two about the relationship between a grandparent and a grandchild. Give your poster a nice slogan.

9 Grandpa Learns to Read and Write

Comprehension

Read this extract from the book 'Little Women' by Louisa May Alcott and answer the questions that follow.

Fortune suddenly smiled upon Jo.

Every few weeks she would shut herself up in her room, put on her scribbling suit and write away at her novel with all her heart and soul, for till that was finished she could find no peace.

She did not think herself a genius by any means, but when the writing fit came on, she gave herself up to it with entire abandon, and led a blissful life, unconscious of want, care, or bad weather, while she sat safe and happy in an imaginary world, full of friends almost as real and dear to her as any in the flesh. Sleep left her eyes, meals stood untasted, day and night were all too short to enjoy the happiness of such times, and made these hours worth living, even if they bore no other fruit.

She was just recovering from one of these attacks when she was asked to escort Miss Crocker to a lecture, on the Pyramids.

They reached early, and Jo amused herself by examining the faces of the people who occupied the seat with them. On her left were two elderly ladies, beyond sat a pair of humble lovers, holding each other by the hand, a sombre spinster eating peppermints, and an old gentleman taking a nap behind a yellow bandanna. On her right, her only neighbour was a studious looking lad absorbed in a newspaper.

It was a pictorial sheet, and Jo examined the work of art nearest her, idly wondering what strange circumstances needed the melodramatic illustration of a chieftain in full war costume, tumbling over a cliff with a wolf at his throat, while two infuriated young gentlemen, with small feet and big eyes, were fighting with swords close by, and a woman was flying away in the background with her mouth wide open. Pausing to turn a page, the lad saw her looking and, with boyish good nature offered half his paper, saying bluntly, 'Want to read it? That's a first-rate story.'

Jo smiled and accepted it, and soon found herself involved in the usual plotline of love, mystery, and murder, for the story belonged to that class of light literature in which the passions have a holiday, and when the author's invention fails, a grand catastrophe clears the stage of one half the dramatis personae, leaving the other half to exult over their downfall.

'Great, isn't it? asked the boy, as her eye went down the last paragraph of her portion.

'I think you and I could do as well as that if we tried,' returned Jo, amused at his admiration of the trash.

'Do you think the author makes a good living out of stories like this?' said Jo.

'Guess she does! She knows just what folks like, and gets paid well for writing it.'

Here the lecture began, but Jo was busy taking down the address of the paper, and resolved to try for the hundred-dollar prize offered in its columns for a sensational story.

She said nothing of her plan at home, but fell to work next day. Jo had never tried this style before. Her story was as full of desperation and despair as her limited acquaintance with those uncomfortable emotions enabled her to make it, and having located it in Lisbon, she wound up with an earthquake, as a striking and appropriate ending. The manuscript was privately dispatched, accompanied by a note, modestly saying that if the tale didn't get the prize, which the writer hardly dared expect, she would be very glad to receive any sum it might be considered worth.

Six weeks is a long time to wait, and Jo was just beginning to give up all hope of ever seeing her manuscript again, when a letter arrived which almost took her breath away, for on opening it, a check for a hundred dollars fell into her lap. For a minute she stared at it, then she read her letter and began to cry. For the letter was encouraging and after years of effort it was so pleasant to find that she had learned to do something, though it was only to write a sensational story.

Letter in one hand, the check in the other, Jo proudly announced to the family that she had won the prize. When the story came, everyone read and praised it, though after her father had told her that the language was good, the romance fresh and hearty, and the tragedy quite thrilling, he shook his head, and said in his unworldly way...

'You can do better than this, Jo. Aim at the highest, and never mind the money.'

A. Spot the words in bold in the passage. Then, underline their meanings.

1. **imaginary**	fantastic	unknown	inexperienced
2. **lecture**	announcement	speech	conversation
3. **modestly**	hopefully	quietly	humbly
4. **unworldly**	carelessly	unthinkingly	innocently
5. **resolved**	calculated	settled	decided

B. Complete these sentences in your own words.

1. Jo was happy when she was writing because ______________________________
______________________________.
2. Jo took down the address of the paper because ______________________________
______________________________.
3. Jo decided to try a new style of writing because ______________________________
______________________________.
4. Jo sent a note with the manuscript because ______________________________
______________________________.
5. Jo's father praised the story because ______________________________
______________________________.

C. Answer the questions with reference to context.

1. *'Great, isn't it?' asked the boy, as her eye went down the last paragraph of her portion.*
   a. Where did Jo meet this boy?
   ____
   ____

b. What did he give Jo to read?

c. What made Jo decide that she wanted to write a similar story?

2. *For a minute she stared, then she read her letter and began to cry.*

a. Why had Jo been waiting eagerly for this letter?

b. Why was the letter more important to her than the money that came with it?

c. What was Jo's father's reaction to the story?

Way with Words

CROSSWORD

A. Complete the crossword below.

Down

1. name of a famous university in England
2. equipment or machinery
4. homonym – weight
6. invented by Alexander Graham Bell
9. on the ____ of the moment

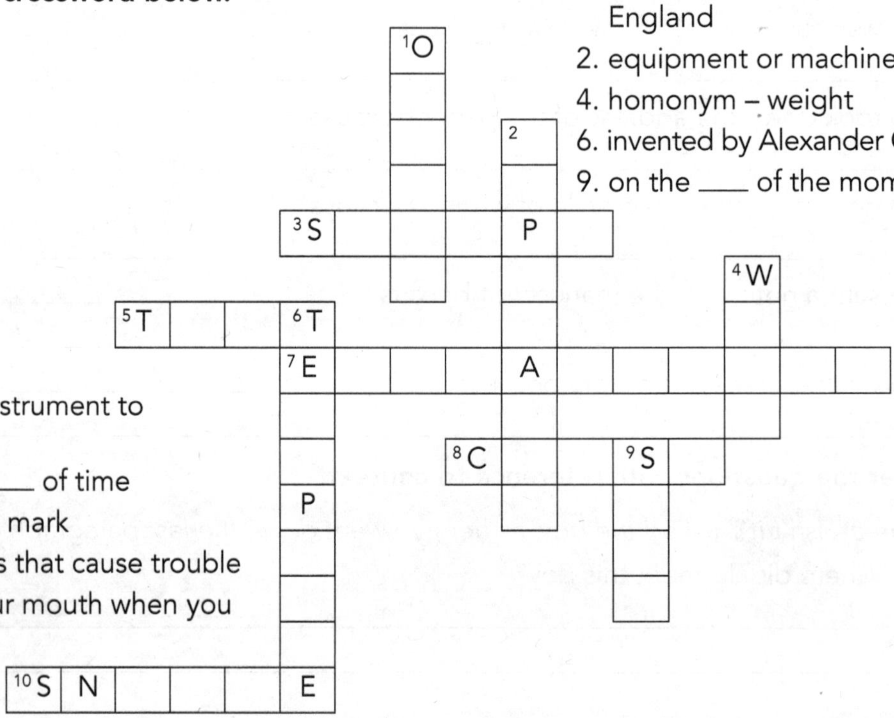

Across

3. use a sharp instrument to remove dirt
5. to stand the ____ of time
7. a punctuation mark
8. magical words that cause trouble
10. you cover your mouth when you do this

Idioms

B. Match the idioms in Column A with their meanings in Column B.

Idioms	Meanings
1. jump on the bandwagon	a. lose control over your actions
2. train of thought	b. express anger
3. blow off steam	c. upset previous plans
4. rock the boat	d. agree with an opinion because it is popular at the moment
5. go off the rails	e. a sequence of reflection

C. Make sentences of your own using the idioms given in exercise B.

1. ____________________
2. ____________________
3. ____________________
4. ____________________
5. ____________________

Grammar in Use

Prepositions

Read these sentences.
I met her **at** the post office.
He sat **beside** her all night.
Here, the words in bold are **prepositions**.

A **preposition** is a word used before a noun or pronoun to show its position, direction, time or movement.

A. Complete the sentences with suitable prepositions.

1. In the last few days, the temperature has gone __________ by ten degrees!
2. I will speak to her __________ the programme is over.
3. The boy swam __________ the river to get help for his ailing mother.
4. Are you going to continue to be negligent __________ your duties towards your family?
5. We will have to climb __________ the fence to get out of the park.

6. Let the prize money be divided equally ____________ all the team members.
7. Could you please get some flowers ____________ the garden?
8. The train ride ____________ the tunnel was exhilarating.

Prepositional Phrases

Read these sentences.

May I pay **by credit card**?
The dog crawled **under the gate** and ran **across the road**.
In these sentences, the groups of words in bold are prepositional phrases.

A **prepositional phrase** is a group of words consisting of a preposition, its object, and any words that modify the object.

B. Underline the prepositional phrases in these sentences.

1. The deer was hunted by the tigress.
2. My parents live on the top floor.
3. Gagan left his clothes in the tub.
4. Mummy made noodles for me.
5. Juhi is the girl in the purple dress.
6. The exhibition included a painting by Hussain.
7. We decided to drive along the Western Ghats.
8. I had a heated debate with my sister.

Listening and Speaking

Read the given quotes.

'If you don't like to read, you haven't found the right book.' – J. K. Rowling

'There is more treasure in a book than all the pirate's loot on treasure island.' – Walt Disney

Discuss them in groups of three and present your ideas in the form of a short speech in class. Each member of the group will give his/her own speech using the points discussed.

Pen it Down

Imagine that your school has changed the mode of learning from print to digital, due to the COVID-19 pandemic. Write a letter to your friend, telling him/her about your experiences with the digital mode of learning.

You can include these points in your letter:

- how the two modes differ
- the advantages and disadvantages of digital learning
- how you plan to keep up with the technological requirements

Test Paper

Comprehension

Read this extract from *Jane Eyre* by Charlotte Bronte and answer the questions that follow.

I tried again to sleep; but my heart beat anxiously: my inward tranquillity was broken. The clock, far down in the hall, struck two. Just then it seemed my chamber door was touched; as if fingers had swept the panels in groping a way along the dark gallery outside. I said, 'Who is there?' Nothing answered. I was chilled with fear.

All at once I remembered that it might be Pilot who, when the kitchen door chanced to be left open, not infrequently found his way up to the threshold of Mr Rochester's chamber. I had seen him lying there myself in the mornings. The idea calmed me somewhat: I lay down. Silence composes the nerves; and as an unbroken hush now reigned again through the whole house, I began to feel the return of slumber. But it was not fated that I should sleep that night.

This was a demonic laugh—low, suppressed and deep—uttered, as it seemed, at the very keyhole of my chamber door. The head of my bed was near the door, and I thought at first the goblin laugher stood at my bedside—or rather, crouched by my pillow: but I rose, looked round, and could see nothing; while, as I still gazed, the unnatural sound was reiterated: and I knew it came from behind the panels. My first impulse was to rise and fasten the bolt; my next, again to cry out, 'Who is there?'

Something gurgled and moaned. Ere long, steps retreated up the gallery towards the third-storey staircase: a door had lately been made to shut in that staircase; I heard it open and close, and all was still.

'Was that Grace Poole? Is she possessed by a devil?' thought I. Impossible now to remain longer by myself: I must go to Mrs Fairfax. I hurriedly put on my frock and a shawl; I withdrew the bolt and opened the door with a trembling hand. There was a candle burning just outside, and on the matting in the gallery. I was surprised at this circumstance: but still more was I amazed to perceive the air quite dim, as if filled with smoke; and, while looking to the right hand and left, I became further aware of a strong smell of burning.

Something creaked: it was a door ajar; and that door was Mr Rochester's, and the smoke rushed in a cloud from thence. I thought no more of Mrs Fairfax; I thought no more of Grace Poole, or the laugh: in an instant, I was within the chamber. Tongues of flame darted round the bed: the curtains were on fire. In the midst of blaze and vapour, Mr Rochester lay stretched motionless, in deep sleep.

'Wake! wake!' I cried. I shook him, but he only murmured and turned: the smoke had stupefied him. Not a moment could be lost. I rushed to his basin and ewer; fortunately, one was wide and the other deep, and both were filled with water. I heaved them up, deluged the bed and its occupant, flew back to my own room, brought my own water jug, baptized the couch afresh, and, by God's aid, succeeded in extinguishing the flames which were devouring it.

1. What is the time mentioned in the passage?

____

____

2. How did the narrator know that someone was there in the room?

____

____

3. Describe the laughter the narrator heard at her keyhole.

____

____

____

4. Whom did the narrator consider responsible for the laugh?

____

____

____

5. What sight greeted the narrator in Mr Rochester's room?

____

____

____

6. How did she try to save Mr Rochester?

____

____

____

Way with Words

A. Form adjectives by adding -ed or -ing to the words given in the box and complete the sentences using them.

encourage	learn	wound	distract	need
overwhelm	embarrass	confuse	fascinate	bore

1. The ____________ noise from the overhead fan made the students restless.
2. The ____________ parents made profuse apologies for their son's behaviour.
3. The ruling party won by an ____________ majority of votes.
4. The ____________ talk given by the coach at halftime lifted the team's morale.
5. The ____________ laser show captivated the audience.
6. This journal usually publishes ____________ articles on the latest scientific advancements.

7. Her mother was moved by the ______________ look on her face and agreed to forgive her mistakes.
8. The construction workers were on a much ______________ break when the manager came to inspect the building site.
9. He looked very ______________ when he was given the directions to the airport.
10. She hated long, ______________ flights and always went to sleep as soon as the plane took off.

B.Complete the following table.

Noun	Verb	Adjective	Adverb
	fear		
	suppressed		X
	amaze		
			surprisingly
silence			
		active	
			prettily

C. Form new words by adding a prefix or a suffix to the words in the brackets. Complete the sentences using these words.

1. Gopi ____________________ (understood) the question and got all the answers wrong.
2. Mary is behaving in a very ____________________ (child) manner.
3. Our school team won the Zonal Table Tennis ____________________. (champion)
4. Our principal does not allow for any form of ____________________ (behaviour) with the teachers.
5. There were only a ____________________ (hand) of people at the church.
6. I want to be a ____________________ (science) when I grow up.
7. Though Susan was discharged from the hospital, she complained about a lot of ____________________. (weak)

D. What do these idioms mean? Choose the correct answer.

1. make ends meet
   a. tie shoe laces ☐
   b. earn enough to sustain ☐
   c. write a short story ☐
2. burn the candles at both ends
   a. make a lamp ☐
   b. long power cuts ☐
   c. work long hours ☐

3. weather a storm
   a. overcome a difficult situation ☐
   b. be critical of someone ☐
   c. step out in bad weather ☐
4. bolt from the blue
   a. to be hit by lightning ☐
   b. to be beaten up ☐
   c. receive a shock ☐
5. get into hot waters
   a. get into trouble ☐
   b. go to a spa ☐
   c. bathe with hot water ☐

Grammar in Use

A. Complete the sentences with suitable prepositions.

1. We could see the fish swim just ____________ the surface of the water.
2. The best time to visit India is usually ____________ September and March.
3. The walk ____________ the seashore was lovely.
4. The tropical countries abound ____________ fruits and flowers.
5. What did you find ____________ the pile of rubble?
6. There were dark patches ____________ her eyes.

B. Rewrite the following paragraph in the simple past tense.

I love chocolates so much that I do not mind having them for breakfast, lunch and dinner. I enjoy the soft and chewy chocolates more than the crunchy ones. I buy chocolates every day from the local grocer who keeps a bar ready for me. It is time to go on a diet!

____

____

____

____

____

____

C. Complete the sentences with the appropriate form of the verbs in the brackets.

1. Surbhi is tired because she ____________ (study) till morning.
2. How many people ____________ (lost) their homes in the earthquake?
3. I ____________ (be) free in the evening today.

4. I __________ (receive) the packet you sent me.
5. I __________ (exercise) for two hours and now I am exhausted.
6. It was late and by the time I reached the shop, it __________ (close) down.
7. Mother __________ (visit) her family in Kolkata.
8. I __________ (take) a flight to Dhaka tomorrow.

D. Rewrite the following sentences according to the instructions given.

1. Oh, what a delicious cake! (Change to an assertive sentence.)

   ____

2. This is not the way to the Governor's House. (Change to an interrogative sentence.)

   ____

3. Quite __________ people are going to arrive early. (Complete using 'few'/'a few'.)

   ____

4. __________ way is the wind blowing? (Complete using a determiner.)

   ____

5. She decided to __________ some money for her daughter's education. (Use a prepositional phrase.)

   ____

6. The Egyptian civilisation is one of the most interesting chapters in history. (Use the comparative form of the adjective.)

   ____

7. The dress is very pretty. (Change into an exclamatory sentence.)

   ____

8. Cars were coming from __________ directions. (Complete using an adjective of quantity.)

   ____

9. What a mess! (Change into an assertive sentence.)

   ____

10. The man, *who was wearing white shoes*, is the hero of this film. (Change the words in italics to a phrase.)

   ____

Listening and Speaking

Choose any one of the following proverbs and present an extempore speech on it.

- Practice makes a person perfect.
- Necessity is the mother of invention.
- Time and tide wait for none.
- As you sow, so you reap.
- A stitch in time saves nine.
- Birds of a feather flock together.

- A bird in hand is worth two in the bush.
- Fortune favours the bold.

Your speech must discuss the meaning of the proverb and why the proverb has become a personal motto for you.

Pen it Down

A. 'Teenagers today are more responsible than their predecessors.' Argue for or against this statement giving suitable reasons for your stand.

B. Imagine that the events in the extract were not caused by a fire but by a ghost. How would it have turned out? Rewrite the extract as a short ghost story and give it a suitable title.

C. Imagine that you have set out on an adventure when you discover you have left an important item behind. Write a letter to your friend, asking him to bring it to you. Remember to mention why that object is so important and how the quest cannot be completed without it.

Travel

10

Dar es Salaam to Nairobi by Ford Prefect

Way with Words

Onomatopoeia

Onomatopoeic words are those containing sounds similar to the noises they describe.

Examples: clash, crash, thud, whizz, splash

A. What sounds do the following make? Fill in the blanks.

1. an angry lion ____________________
2. car stuck in a traffic ____________________
3. waves crashing on the shore ____________________
4. a fan ____________________
5. a clock ____________________
6. church bells ____________________

Word Search

B. Find the answers to these questions in the grid below.

1. Is a shy person also called *different* or *diffident*?
2. Which character trait is more negative, *impetuous* or *rash*?
3. Is a proud person *pushy* or *haughty*?
4. A person who is nervous can also be called ____________________
5. Which word is a better way of saying *talkative*?

S	S	D	F	G	H	J	K	L	O
U	D	I	F	F	I	D	E	N	T
O	F	F	G	G	J	D	A	I	S
L	W	S	R	K	F	S	Z	Y	S
U	W	H	A	U	G	H	T	Y	D
R	E	F	S	J	S	U	C	U	F
R	S	V	H	G	X	I	V	H	X
A	P	O	I	U	T	K	H	S	C
G	F	S	K	I	T	T	I	S	H

Grammar in Use

INFINITIVES

Read these sentences.

I wanted **to play** football.

He continued **to study** hard.

In the above sentences, the groups of words in bold are **infinitives**.

An **infinitive** is a non-finite verb, formed by the addition of *to* before the base form of a verb.

A. Join the following sentences using infinitives.

1. He went to the library. He was looking for a book on ancient civilisations.
2. The teacher asked for a sheet of chart paper. She wanted to draw the diagrams.
3. We are going on a field trip. We have a project to complete.
4. Sally was excited. She had been chosen as the Head Girl.
5. I was very enthusiastic. I wanted to volunteer for the job.

TRANSFORMATION OF SENTENCES USING INFINITIVES

We can change a complex sentence to a simple sentence using infinitives.

Example: The children were delighted when they saw the bags of candies. (complex)
The children were delighted **to see** the bags of candies. (simple)

B. Rewrite the following sentences using infinitives.

1. I found walking with the giraffes exhilarating.
2. The tug-of-war participants began pulling in opposite directions.
3. I stopped and watched the seagulls frolic.
4. The environment needs protection.

5. Our attitude towards the underprivileged need changing.

6. It was a wise decision giving up gossiping.

Gerunds

Read the given sentence.

Reading storybooks is Mohini's favourite pastime.

In the sentence, the word in bold is a **gerund**.

A **gerund** is a non-finite verb that acts like a noun. It takes the *-ing* form of the verb. They can act as the subject or object of a verb.

C. Identify the gerunds in the following sentences.

1. She delayed submitting her assignment.
2. I miss visiting museums with my family.
3. They could not help staring at her orange-coloured shoes.
4. I really cannot stand waiting for her to arrive.
5. We postponed the shooting of the film.
6. Swimming in a torrid river is dangerous.
7. Keeping secrets from family members is not beneficial.
8. Jogging everyday in the morning will keep you fit and healthy.

Listening and Speaking

Listen to a passage about Ladakh and answer the questions that follow.

1. What kind of landscape surrounds Leh?

2. What makes the city of Leh unique?

3. Where are the hot springs located?

4. Which lake do the migratory birds visit?

5. Which area of Ladakh has fewer tourists?

6. How has Buddhism influenced the people of this region?

Pen it Down

Write a letter to the editor of your local newspaper about the poor implementation of fire safety measures in a famous tourist spot in your neighbourhood.

11

Uncle Alfred's Long Jump

Way with Words

IRONY

Read this sentence.

Mary Ann stepped out in the terrible blizzard and remarked, 'What lovely weather!'

Here, Mary Ann's remark is **ironical**—the weather is obviously not pleasant or lovely.

Irony is one of the most commonly used techniques of writing in which the writer deliberately states the opposite of what is happening, to create humour.

Irony is different from sarcasm which has a harsher tone to it.

A. Fill in the blanks with groups of words that make the following sentences ironic.

1. The wedding guest is on his fifth serving of ice cream. He comments,
   '______________________________'
2. The television channel is showing the re-run of the same series for the 3rd year in a row. Deborah remarks,
   '______________________________'
3. The policeman was caught violating traffic rules. The newspaper headline stated
   '______________________________'
4. Martha hit her head on the bathroom door, walked into a window and split coffee on her shirt. She blurted out,
   '______________________________'
5. The BTS concert was almost sold out and Kaylie was desperate for tickets. She said,
   '______________________________'
6. The senior student was not able to explain the chapter very well and the junior student remarked,
   '______________________________'

Proverbs

Read these sentences.

Early to bed and early to rise, makes a man healthy, wealthy and wise.

Laugh and the world laughs with you, weep and you weep alone.

These are **proverbs**. Proverbs are short, crisp sayings that give advice or tell us something about life.

B. Read the given meanings. Fill in the blanks with suitable proverbs.

1. Doing things on time helps save time.

   ____

2. Be careful before you take any action.

   ____

3. It is futile getting upset over what has already happened.

   ____

4. What you possess is more valuable than what you plan to possess.

   ____

5. An irresponsible person will always blame others for his/her own inefficiency.

   ____

6. What you do tells others more about you than your words.

   ____

Grammar in Use

Coordinating and Subordinating Conjunctions

Read these sentences.

It's a small car, **yet** it's surprisingly spacious.

My hand was still hurting, **so** I went to see a doctor.

In these sentences, the words in bold are **coordinating conjunctions.**

A conjunction that joins two sentences or clauses of equal importance is called a **coordinating conjunction**. Some common coordinating conjunctions are **and, but, or, for, yet, neither, so** and **still.**

A. Complete the sentences using the appropriate coordinating conjunctions. Some of them may be repeated.

so	or	and	but	for	yet

1. He keeps falling sick, ____________ he does not take his medicines on time.
2. I was ravenous, ____________ I ate up the whole cake.
3. He is poor ____________ trustworthy.
4. He does not drink tea ____________ coffee.
5. He ran to the bus stop, ____________ he still missed the bus.
6. You should try to help him ____________ he is your oldest friend.
7. I want to go home early ____________ watch the football match.
8. I have just eaten lunch ____________ I am not hungry at all.

Read the sentences.

It's twenty years **since** I've seen her.

If anyone calls, tell them I'm not at home.

Here, the words in bold are **subordinating conjunctions.**

A conjunction that connects a dependent clause with an independent clause is called a **subordinating conjunction**. Some common subordinating conjunctions are **while, as, because, since, until, although, even though, as soon as** and **so that.**

B. Complete the sentences with suitable subordinating conjunctions.

1. I am not letting you go ____________ you apologise for your behaviour.
2. She is rushing through the job ____________ she can meet the deadline.
3. Sarah has not called even once ____________ she shifted to Mumbai.
4. ____________ she is of poor health, she tries her best to work hard.
5. Everyone's eyes were on him ____________ he continued with his speech.
6. We need to work hard ____________ we want to pass the exam.
7. Everyone likes Ray ____________ he is so nice and helpful.
8. ____________ she went to the grocery store, she didn't buy anything.

Indefinite Pronouns

Look at the sentences.

Everyone cheered and clapped.

Nobody knew what to say.

In these sentences, the words in bold are **indefinite pronouns.**

Indefinite pronouns are those that refer to a person or a thing without saying exactly who or what they are.

C. Fill in the blanks with indefinite pronouns.

anything	everything	anybody	nobody	something	someone	nothing

1. There is ____________ in my eye. I need to wash it.
2. The witness could share ____________ useful with the detectives.
3. Ramesh was punished though he didn't do ____________ wrong.
4. We had a great holiday; ____________ was perfect.
5. When I reached home, ____________ was there.
6. I am sure I left my book here. Could ____________ have taken it?
7. Not saying ____________ is better than saying something rude.

Listening and Speaking

Which of the two – luck or talent – helps one succeed? Have a class discussion on the subject.

You can talk about the following points:

- Luck holds no meaning without talent.
- Talent coupled with luck is a great combination.

Pen it Down

Imagine that you are a special correspondent for a daily newspaper. You witnessed an Olympic sporting event where a sportsperson broke a world record. Write a news report, describing what happened and how you felt watching it happen in front of your eyes.

Science Fiction

12
The Invisible Man

Way with Words

Figurative Language

Read this line.

Reya sang **as sweetly as a bird**.

Here, the simile **as sweetly as a bird** is used as part of **figurative language** to indicate how melodiously Reya sang, by comparing the sweetness of her voice to that of a bird.

Now, read this phrase.

the clatter of feet about me

Here, the word 'clatter' indicates the sound of the feet around the speaker, creating a specific effect of crowding.

Writers use a variety of techniques to create special effects in their writing. **Figurative language** is one such technique. It involves using language in a way that goes beyond the literal meaning of words. Figurative language makes use of similes, metaphors, alliteration, onomatopoeia, assonance and a variety of other literary devices.

A. Underline the instances of figurative language in these sentences. Explain them in your own words.

1. The rocket whizzed past my ear dangerously.

___

___

2. Her silent scream echoed through the universe.

___

___

3. She sailed down the corridor with an air of confidence.

___

___

4. The lazy leopard lounged near the lake.

___

___

5. Solving this sum is as easy as eating cake!

____

____

6. The mighty cloud roared at the mountain.

____

____

NOMINALISATION

You have learnt that nominalisation helps to make writing more crisp and precise. They are nouns created from verbs or adjectives.

Examples:

The government **is enforcing** Covid protocols very strictly. (verb)
There is strict **enforcement** of Covid protocols. (noun)
It is necessary that we **amplify** this issue. (verb)
Amplification of this issue is necessary. (noun)

B. Rewrite the following sentences after changing the underlined words to their noun forms.

1. This map needs to be <u>modified</u>.

____

2. Do not <u>glorify</u> overworking at the cost of health.

____

3. She <u>prepared</u> methodically for the examination.

____

4. It is essential to <u>cancel</u> all travel plans now.

____

5. They want the issue of ration and medicine distribution to be <u>resolved</u>.

____

6. You should <u>nourish</u> your body with a good diet.

____

Grammar in Use

PRESENT AND PAST PARTICIPLES

You know that participles are a type of non-finite verbs.

Present participles refer to incomplete actions or states of being. These are formed by adding *-ing* to the base form of the verbs.

Example: We woke up early to watch the **rising** sun.

Past participles refer to actions that have been completed in the past but whose effects still remain. These are formed by adding *-ed*, *-en*, *-d*, *-t* or *-n* to the base form of the verbs.

Example: Please repair the **broken** window.

A. Underline the present participles in the following sentences.

1. Neha is known for her caring nature.
2. Please keep an eye on the boiling water.
3. It was an amazing experience.
4. He found himself trapped in a burning train.
5. They looked at the flying birds.
6. The running water soothed our nerves.
7. The crying baby could not be consoled.
8. The falling snow added to the magic of Christmas Eve.
9. The screaming woman ran out of the haunted house.
10. The fading colours of the painting revealed a message written beneath it.

B. Complete the phrases with the past participle form of verbs in the brackets. One is done for you.

1. *astonished* audience (astonish)
2. __________ shoes (wash)
3. __________ readers (fascinate)
4. __________ questions (forget)
5. __________ students (confuse)
6. __________ parents (worry)
7. __________ trousers (alter)
8. __________ watches (steal)
9. __________ papers (solve)
10. __________ disputes (resolve)

ACTIVE AND PASSIVE VOICE

Read these sentences.

My mother bakes a cake every Friday. (active voice)
A cake is baked by my mother every Friday. (passive voice)

In the **active voice**, the subject is the doer of the action.
In the **passive voice**, the subject is acted upon.

C. **Identify if the sentences are in the active or passive voice and then rewrite them in the other voice. One is done for you.**

1. The masons are building the church. (active voice)
   This church is being built by the masons. (passive voice)
2. They were duped by the travelling robbers.
3. I was taught Hindi by a well-known writer.
4. The children are finishing the project quickly.
5. By whom was this vase broken?
6. Did Rowan bring these books from the library?
7. The last batsman won the match for our team.
8. The rats were enchanted by the tune played by the Pied Piper and followed him as he went towards the river.

Listening and Speaking

You need your friend's help to complete your art project on time. In pairs, enact a conversation where you request your friend to help you out.

You may use the following sentence starters:

- Can I ask you for a favour?
- Would you help me with…?
- Do you have any ideas regarding…?
- Can we work together on…?

Pen it Down

Look up the Internet and collect information about a famous travel writer whom you admire. Then, write an essay on him/her.

Include the following information in your essay:

- facts about the writer
- the places he/she has written about
- what makes his/her writing special
- which location described by him/her you would like to visit

13 The Model Millionaire

Comprehension

Read the following extract from 'Three Men in a Boat' by Jerome K. Jerome and answer the questions that follow.

What I suffer in that way no tongue can tell. From my earliest infancy, I have been a martyr to it. As a boy, the disease hardly ever left me for a day. They did not know then that it was my liver. Medical science was in a far less advanced state than now, and they used to put it down to laziness.

'Why, you skulking little devil, you,' they would say, 'get up and do something for your living, can't you?'—not knowing, of course, that I was ill.

And they didn't give me pills; they gave me clumps on the side of the head. And, strange as it may appear, those clumps on the head often cured me—for the time being. I have known one clump on the head have more effect upon my liver, and make me feel more anxious to go straight away then and there, and do what was wanted to be done, without further loss of time, than a whole box of pills does now.

You know, it often is so—those simple, old-fashioned remedies are sometimes more efficacious than all the dispensary stuff.

We sat there for half-an-hour, describing to each other our maladies. I explained to George and William Harris how I felt when I got up in the morning, and William Harris told us how he felt when he went to bed; and George stood on the hearthrug, and gave us a clever and powerful piece of acting, illustrative of how he felt in the night.

George fancies he is ill, but there's never anything really the matter with him, you know.

At this point, Mrs Poppets knocked at the door to know if we were ready for supper. We smiled sadly at one another, and said we supposed we had better try to swallow a bit. Harris said a little something in one's stomach often kept the disease in check; and Mrs Poppets brought the tray in, and we drew up to the table, and toyed with a little steak and onions, and some rhubarb tart.

I must have been very weak at the time, because I know, after the first half-hour or so, I seemed to take no interest whatever in my food—an unusual thing for me—and I didn't want any cheese.

This duty done, we refilled our glasses and resumed the discussion upon our state of health. What it was that was actually the matter with us, none of us could be sure of, but the unanimous opinion was that it—whatever it was—had been brought on by overwork.

'What we want is rest,' said Harris.

'Rest and a complete change,' said George. 'The overstrain upon our brains has produced a general depression throughout the system. Change of scene and absence of the necessity for thought will restore the mental equilibrium.'

George has a cousin who is usually described in the charge sheet as a medical student. So, he naturally has a somewhat family-physicianary way of putting things.

I agreed with George and suggested that we should seek out some retired and old-world spot, far from the madding crowd, and dream away a sunny week among its drowsy lanes—some half-forgotten nook, hidden away by the fairies, out of reach of the noisy world—some quaint-perched eyrie on the cliffs of Time, from whence the surging waves of the nineteenth century would sound far-off and faint.

Harris said, 'If you want rest and change, you can't beat a sea trip.'

1. Which disease did the narrator have during his childhood?

___

2. Which remedy was he given?

___

3. Who were the narrator's friends?

___

4. What did the friends think the reason for their illness was?

___

5. What impact did their illness have on their appetite?

___

6. What according to them would cure the illness?

___

7. Find words from the extract which mean the same as the following:
   a. frail: ___
   b. balance: ___
   c. diseases: ___
   d. efficient: ___

Way with Words

Antonyms

A. Fill in the blanks with antonyms of the given words.

1. behave: ____________
2. relevant: ____________
3. clear: ____________
4. essential: ____________
5. respect: ____________
6. similar: ____________
7. pronounce: ____________
8. communicate: ____________
9. appear: ____________
10. mortal: ____________

B. Choose the best alternative to complete the following sentences.

1. The Titanic sailed on its maiden ____________ (flight/journey/voyage) in 1912.
2. The ____________ (keen/courteous/civilised) young man escorted us into the hall.
3. His ____________ (exorbitant/exceeding/extreme) kindness to his students made him a universal favourite.
4. ____________ (Exotic/Strange/Unfamiliar) things have been happening next door since the new neighbours moved in.
5. The detective could ____________ (guess/discern/watch) a faint outline of a footprint on the wet ground.

Grammar in Use

Modals

Read these sentences.

Change of scene and absence of the necessity for thought **will** restore the mental equilibrium.

I suggested that we **should** seek out some retired and old-world spot.

We **must** respect our elders.

Here, the words **will**, **should** and **must** are modals.

Modals are a type of auxiliary or helping verbs.

They are used to express necessity, ability, possibility, advice, permission, suggestion, future action and request.

A. Complete the sentences with the correct modals from the box.

shouldn't	needn't	mustn't	might	can't

1. I ________________ do more than one round of cartwheels.
2. Sharp objects ________________ be kept within the reach of children.
3. People ________________ touch the wet paint on the benches in the park.
4. It ________________ get difficult for you to remember all these details.
5. You ________________ buy those expensive shoes if they are beyond your budget.

TRANSFORMATION OF SENTENCES USING *IF* AND *UNLESS*

Read this sentence.

If you want rest and change, you can't beat a sea trip.

In the above sentence, the word 'if' represents a condition, based on which the situation mentioned in the sentence follows.

It can be rewritten as:

Unless you go on a sea trip, you won't get rest and change.

Such sentences are known as **conditional sentences** as they express a certain situation which is determined by certain conditions.

B. Rewrite the following sentences as directed.

1. If you see a crowd outside the mall, be sure that the film star has arrived. (Begin with 'unless'.)

   ____

2. Unless you have been invited, you will not be allowed to enter the premises. (Begin with 'if'.)

   ____

3. It is going to rain. We shall not play outside. (Join the two sentences beginning with 'if'.)

   ____

4. Unless the principal gives permission, there will be no football matches this term. (Begin with 'if'.)

   ____

5. If the morning assembly goes off well, the teachers will be very happy. (Begin with 'unless'.)

   ____

6. The dog may bite. It must be given food. (Join the two sentences beginning with 'if'.)

   ____

Listening and Speaking

We respond to changes in our natural and social environment. How would the following changes affect you?

- Your school is moving to a new locality.
- Your doctor puts you on a strict diet to improve your health.
- Your elder brother leaves home and starts college in a different city.
- The government decides to impose a heavy tax on fast food restaurants.

Use these phrases to talk to your partner about these situations.

- I would be quite upset because…
- It wouldn't affect me much because…
- I would be really delighted if…
- It would be wonderful if…
- I will be able to do so many things if…
- It's for my own good if…
- I would be so sad if…

Pen it Down

Imagine that you have won a lottery suddenly. Write a diary entry expressing your feelings and what you plan to do with your winnings.

14 The Human Seasons

Way with Words

Idioms

Certain situations have been given. Write the most appropriate idiom for each situation. One is done for you.

1. I have sent him my resignation letter. *The die has been cast*. (Hint: Something irreversible has already been done.)
2. 'This is my final offer. Now, the ball ______________________.' (Hint: It is up to you to take the next step.)
3. 'Can you really do two projects in one week and also manage to go for tennis and guitar practice? Don't bite ______________________.' (Hint: To take on a task that is too big to achieve.)
4. My classmates and I disagree on the concept of free will. We don't ______________________. (Hint: To not agree with someone over something.)
5. He said 'no' even before he had heard her complete her sentence. As a result of his ______________________, he missed out on a good opportunity. (Hint: A reaction made without examining the situation, cause or facts.)

Grammar in Use

Main and Subordinate Clauses

Look at this sentence.

He had just drifted off to sleep when the phone rang.

Here, the group of words in bold makes complete sense on its own. It is a **main clause**. The underlined group of words cannot stand on its own and is therefore a **subordinate clause**.

A clause that has a finite verb and a subject, and makes complete sense by itself is called a **main clause**.

A clause that has a finite verb and a subject, and depends on the main clause for its meaning, is called a **subordinate clause**.

Underline the main clause and circle the subordinate clause in each of these sentences.

1. As we were late for the performance, we had to wait in the long queue to get in.
2. If he asks you for your pencil, it means that he has lost his yet again.
3. We found the dog exactly where we had left her.
4. The doctor arrived after the patient was rushed to the operation theatre.
5. I will fight to the finish because I do not believe in giving up easily.
6. He took off his shoes while entering so that he didn't make any noise.
7. Mary realised that she had left her ticket at home when she reached the station.
8. The girl, who is wearing the pink pyjamas, is my sister.

Listening and Speaking

You have learnt about rising and falling intonation. Now, read the following rules.

- For yes/no questions, use a **rising intonation** (↑) at the end of the sentence.
- For most other types of *wh-* questions, use a **falling intonation** (↓) at the end of the sentence.
- Most regular statements which state facts or information use a **falling intonation** (↓) at the end of the sentence.
- Items on a list use a **rising intonation** (↑) until the final item, which uses a **falling intonation** (↓).
- High-energy emotions like happiness, excitement, fright and annoyance usually use a **rising intonation** (↑).
- Use **rising intonation** (↑) on questions at the end of a sentence which require clarification or opinion from your speaking partner. These are called **tag questions**.

Remember that proper intonation is important to convey the right tone or emotion in a sentence.

Read these lines aloud. Mark the words that have rising intonation with an upward arrow (↑) and those that show falling intonation with a downward arrow (↓).

1. Have you completed your work?
2. Why are you refusing to answer my question?
3. I have been swimming for the school team for two years.
4. I love having grapes, mangoes and watermelons on a hot day.
5. I can't believe that he refused to let you borrow his scooter!
6. This is a tiring journey, isn't it?

Pen it Down

Write a poem on your favourite family member. You can write about the following points in your poem:

- introduction of the family member
- why he/she is your favourite
- memorable moments spent with him/her

15

Miss Smith and the Black Pearl

Comprehension

Read the passage and answer the questions that follow.

When December 1, 1955 dawned on Montgomery in Alabama, little did anyone residing in the United States of America ever know that it was going to be one of the most historical moments for the nation. That Thursday became immortalised as the day when a simple lady began a chain reaction of protests against racial discrimination by simply refusing to give up her seat to a white man, even after threats of arrest. Rosa Parks refused to comply with the unjust Jim Crow laws of segregation of races on buses and rewrote years of quiet surrender to racial discrimination in every sphere of American life.

According to the laws, Black people were not allowed to occupy the front seats of a bus. Rosa Parks, a 42-year-old seamstress, was sitting in the front row of the seats meant for the Blacks but which could be occupied by Whites in case their seats were full. When the bus driver asked her to vacate her seat for a white man, she refused.

According to Parks, the real reason for her rebellion was that she felt she had the right to be treated fairly and was tired of suffering this kind of unfair treatment for so long like the other members of her community. She said, 'People always say that I didn't give up my seat because I was tired, but that isn't true. I was not tired physically … No, the only tired I was, was tired of giving in.'

A few days after the protest, on December 5, 1955, Parks was arrested, jailed and fined. This action sparked off a major civil rights action movement in the country including a bus boycott that lasted for over 381 days, known as the 'Montgomery Bus Boycott'. The protest movement was headed by civil rights activist Reverend Martin Luther King Jr.

Rosa Parks had been a long-time civil rights activist. In the aftermath of her protest, she lost her job and was harassed and threatened. In November 1956, almost after a year since the incident, the Supreme Court of the country declared the bus segregation laws as unconstitutional. Parks came to be celebrated as the 'Mother of the Civil rights movement in America'

Though her stand was proved right, she had to shift to Detroit with her family in view of the threat to her life, in 1958. She worked throughout her life for equal rights and went on to establish the Rosa and Raymond Parks Institute for Self-Development in 1987.

Parks was awarded the Presidential Medal of Freedom and then the Congressional Gold Medal in 1997.

Rosa Parks was known as a woman of courage and piety. The equal rights activist stands tall even today as the symbol of the power of a single individual to effect changes in society.

Her legacy remains tied to these words – *'I would like to be remembered as a person who wanted to be free … so other people would also be free.'*

The world we live in today has seen great social and cultural changes since Rosa Parks began her struggle for equal rights. However, racism and intolerance still continue in all societies. In recent times, the Black Lives Matter movement has rallied together thousands of young people globally to protest against injustice and violence still inflicted on people of colour. This movement, which spread at first through social media, has forced institutions and individuals to start difficult conversations about race relations.

A. State whether the given sentences are true (T) or false (F). Correct the false sentences.

1. Rosa Parks could not find a seat on the bus. ☐
2. The Jim Crow laws supported segregation. ☐
3. Rosa Parks was asked to vacate a seat for a white man. ☐
4. Rosa Parks was tired, so she did not want to give up her seat. ☐
5. The Montgomery Bus Boycott was to support Rosa Parks' action. ☐
6. The US Supreme Court has abolished the law segregating people on buses. ☐
7. Rosa Parks lost her job after being jailed. ☐
8. Social media has not helped the Black Lives Matter movement. ☐

B. Complete the following sentences in your own words.

1. The bus driver asked Rosa Parks to vacate the seat because ____________________
____
____.
2. Rosa Parks was jailed, arrested and fined for ____________________
____
____.
3. Rosa Parks was awarded the Presidential Medal of Freedom because ____________________
____
____.
4. Thousands of young people have joined the Black Lives Matter movement because
____
____.

Way with Words

Homographs

Homographs are words which are similar in spelling but have different meanings.

Example: The little **swallow** perched itself on the branch. (bird)
I could not **swallow** the bitter medicine easily. (to ingest)

A. Frame sentences with the following homographs, using them in a way that their differences in meaning are clearly indicated.

1. wind

2. bear

3. lead

4. reason

5. fair

6. bow

7. minute

B. Choose the correct homonyms to complete the sentences.

1. The new ______________ (steel/steal) safe in the bank drew everyone's attention.
2. The thin ______________ (pane/pain) of glass shook as the fierce storm raged outside.
3. To make a good cake, you have to ensure that the ______________ (dough/doe) rises well.
4. The captain of the team was down with ______________ (flu/flew) and so the vice-captain had to take over.
5. During the ______________ (reign/rein) of Akbar, there was ______________ (peace/piece) and prosperity throughout the county.
6. The boat passed through a narrow ______________ (straight/strait).
7. The ball went right ______________ (threw/through) the window.
8. If one of the countries ______________ (breaks/brakes) the treaty, there will be war.

C. Form sentences with these pairs of homonyms to bring out the difference in their meanings. Use a dictionary if required.

1. ewe, you

____

____

2. sheer, shear

____

____

3. jeans, genes

____

____

Grammar in Use

Simple, Compound and Complex Sentences

A **simple sentence** has only a single independent clause **and** no dependent clause.

Example: Rosa Parks had been a long-time civil rights activist.

A **compound sentence** has two independent clauses joined using a coordinating conjunction.

Example: She worked throughout her life for equal rights **and** went on to establish the Rosa and Raymond Parks Institute for Self Development in 1987.

A **complex sentence** has an independent clause and one or more dependent clauses. These are usually joined by a subordinating conjunction or a relative pronoun.

Example: **When** the bus driver asked her to vacate her seat for a white man, she refused.

A. Identify the following sentences as simple (S), compound (C) or complex (CO).

1. The rooms smell of phenyl and moth balls. ______
2. Most of the sportsmen are from poor backgrounds and have worked hard to make it to the team. ______
3. The students started working eagerly on the project when they heard about the prize. ______
4. The villagers were invited to the meet but they refused to attend the rally. ______
5. While everyone was busy at home, I went and did the shopping. ______
6. My parents will be going for a wedding tonight but I will stay home. ______
7. I will attend a new school soon. ______
8. My new school, which is in the mountains, is known for its sporting achievements. ______

B. Join these pairs of simple sentences to form compound and complex sentences.

1. I wrote a long essay. It was in simple language.
____
2. Sita is my friend. Deb is my friend too.
____
3. Shall we stay at home? Shall we go to the park?
____
4. James came home late. His parents had already had dinner by then.
____
5. Peter does not want to buy a new car. Peter does not want to buy a scooter.
____
6. Susan studied hard all night. She did not do too well in the test.
____
7. A man was found snooping around the bank. The police arrested him.
____
8. I had to buy my friend a present. I went to the gift shop.
____

Adjective Clauses

You have learnt that there are three types of clauses.

Read this sentence.

This is the seat **which Rosa Parks did not give up**.

Here, the group of words forms an **adjective clause**.

An **adjective clause** performs the function of an adjective in a sentence. It modifies the noun in the main clause.

C. Choose the correct adjective clause to complete each sentence.

1. The boy, ________________, has been given a scholarship for higher studies.
   a. after receiving the award for bravery b. who received the award for bravery
2. The house, ________________, is under renovation.
   a. which is around the corner b. where is around the corner
3. Time, ________________, is the most powerful thing in the world.
   a. waiting for no man b. which waits for no man
4. She wants the bag ________________.
   a. which her best friend was carrying. b. in the window shop.
5. The villa, ________________, is rumoured to be haunted.
   a. which was built by the Bourbon dynasty b. belonging to the Bourbon dynasty

Listening and Speaking

Tell your friends about your favourite film or television show. You can talk about the following points:

- the plot of the show
- the time period the show or film is set in
- the actors and who your favourite among them is
- what you like the most about the film or the show

Pen it Down

Write a letter to your pen-friend describing the most beautiful season in your city. Give reasons for your choice of season. Describe the unique changes that take place in your city at the onset of the season.

16 Unbreakable

Comprehension

Read an extract from the poem 'If' by Rudyard Kipling and answer the questions that follow.

If you can keep your head when all about you
Are losing theirs and blaming it on you;
If you can trust yourself when all men doubt you,
But make allowance for their doubting too:
If you can wait and not be tired by waiting,
Or, being lied about, don't deal in lies,
Or being hated don't give way to hating,
And yet don't look too good, nor talk too wise;

If you can talk with crowds and keep your virtue,
Or walk with Kings—nor lose the common touch,
If neither foes nor loving friends can hurt you,
If all men count with you, but none too much:
If you can fill the unforgiving minute
With sixty seconds' worth of distance run,
Yours is the Earth and everything that's in it,
And—which is more—you'll be a Man, my son!

1. Why do you think the poem is titled 'If'?

2. What does the phrase 'to keep one's head' mean?

3. What does the poet mean by the term 'allowance'? How can we 'make allowance' for the 'doubting' of others?

4. What message does the poet try to convey through these lines?
Or, being lied about, don't deal in lies,
Or being hated don't give way to hating,

5. What do the phrases, 'walk with Kings' and not 'lose the common touch' mean?

6. What, according to you, is the central message of this poem?

Way with Words

EXPRESSIONS RELATED TO SPORTS

Sports is a vast sphere of activity which has produced many expressions. These are now used to indicate different kinds of situations in life as well.

Example: to give (something) your best shot
This means to try one's best. It first originated in sporting activities connected to shooting.

Match the following sports expressions with their meanings. Also, guess the name of the sport from which each originated.

Expression	Meaning
1. be out of someone's league	a. always be prepared
2. stay ahead of the game	b. give up
3. hit below the belt	c. you are responsible for taking action now
4. throw in the towel	d. be proactive and take charge
5. the ball is in your court	e. not be at par with someone else
6. take the bull by its horns	f. hurt someone intentionally

Grammar in Use

Noun and Adverb Clauses

You have earlier learnt about adjective clauses. There are two more types of clauses – adverb and noun.

An **adverb clause** is a subordinate clause that performs the function of an adverb. It modifies a verb, an adjective or another adverb.

Adverb clauses can be of manner, time, place and reason.

Examples: He spoke **as if he had no idea of what had happened.** (manner)
People were worried **when they heard about the pandemic.** (time)
I am meeting my cousins at the place **where the fair is being held.** (place)
He could not sit for the exams **because he was ill.** (reason)

A **noun clause** is a subordinate clause that performs the function of a noun in a sentence. It can be the subject, the object or the complement of the verb.

It is usually introduced by the word **that**, and relative pronouns like **what**, **why**, and others.

Examples: We expect **that they will come home tonight.**
I cannot understand **why you are lying about this matter.**

A. Identify the underlined clauses as noun clause (NC) or adverb clause (AC).

1. As it was a sunny day, the children decided to go on a field trip to the zoo. ______
2. That he was going to join the new company was known to all. ______
3. We will complete the syllabus after the school reopens in June. ______
4. The monkeys were sure that the lion would not return to frighten them. ______
5. She danced as if she was listening to some heavenly music only she could hear. ______
6. We don't know whether the library will be open today. ______
7. They went wherever they had been instructed to. ______

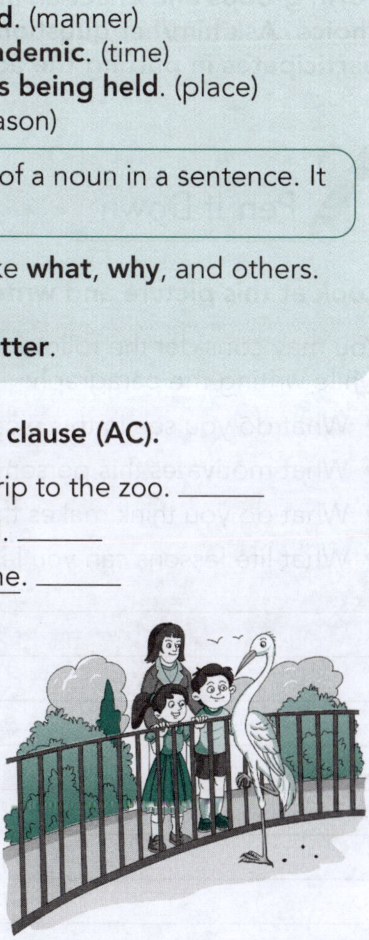

B. Complete these sentences with suitable noun clauses.

1. The king ordered ____________________
2. He said ____________________
3. I cannot believe ____________________
4. We know ____________________

C. Complete these sentences with suitable adverb clauses.

1. I waited for my sister ____________________
2. Saurav finished his work early ____________________
3. Close the door ____________________
4. He doesn't speak French ____________________

Listening and Speaking

Form groups and enact an interview between a reporter and a famous person of your choice. Ask him/her questions about his/her life. Make sure each member of the group participates in putting the act together.

Pen it Down

Look at this picture and write two paragraphs on it.

You may consider the following questions while writing the paragraph:

- What do you see in this picture?
- What motivates this person to take part in this activity?
- What do you think makes the sport special?
- What life lessons can you learn from this sportsperson?

17

At the Theatre: To the Lady Behind Me

Way with Words

Idioms with *Play*

A. Make sentences with the following idioms with 'play'.

1. play it by ear

____

2. be child's play

____

3. a play on words

____

B. Match the phrasal verbs with their correct meanings.

A	B
1. play false	a. act in a generally accepted manner
2. play cool	b. act without help
3. play for time	c. to cheat someone
4. play a lone hand	d. use delaying tactics
5. play by the rules	e. make a contribution to something
6. play a part	f. pretend to be calm

Collective Nouns

You know that **collective nouns** are names assigned to a group of people or things considered a single entity.

Examples: a **school** of fish, a **pod** of dolphins, a **pride** of lions

C. Match the nouns in column A with the collective nouns associated with them in column B.

A	B
1. rubbish	a. choir
2. singers	b. catalogue
3. films	c. anthology
4. prices	d. gaggle
5. poems	e. heap
6. geese	f. reel

Grammar in Use

Position of Adverbs

A. Insert the following adverbs in their correct places and rewrite the sentences.

1. He drove the car into the garage. (carefully)
   ____
2. I will give you the important details. (tomorrow)
   ____
3. I go for walks in the evenings. (often)
   ____
4. She doesn't play tennis in the mornings. (always)
   ____
5. He decided to stay. (behind)
   ____

Adverb Phrases

Read this sentence.

Sakshi unwrapped the gift <u>with great excitement</u>.

In the above sentence, the underlined group of words describe the manner in which Sakshi unwrapped the gift, and is therefore, an **adverb phrase**.

Adverb phrases, like adverbs, modify or describe verbs. They answer the questions *how*, *where*, *when*, *how often* and *why* something happened.

B. Underline the adverb phrases in these sentences.

1. Sneha parked her car in the garage.
2. We played football on the beach.

3. Mother looked at Bruno with a stern expression.
4. The children play all day long.
5. Let's plan to meet on Friday.
6. I go cycling every weekend.
7. The tourists walked in a hurried manner to look at the high waves.
8. You should always revise your answers with care.

Transformation of Sentences with Adverb Phrases

You have learnt that a sentence with an adverb phrase can be rewritten using an adverb, and vice versa.

Example: She donated money **generously**. (adverb)
She donated money **in a generous manner**. (adverb phrase)

C. Replace the adverb phrases in these sentences with adverbs that mean the same.

1. She performed the task with much skill.
2. The guns went off with a lot of noise.
3. All of a sudden, she felt very scared.
4. A notorious troll lives in this place.
5. They stopped to take rest at that time.

Transformation of Simple, Complex and Compound Sentences

You have learnt that a simple sentence can be converted to a compound sentence by extending a word or phrase to form an independent clause.

Example: Besides comforting the child, he also fed her. (simple)
He not only comforted the child but he also fed her. (compound)

A simple sentence can also be converted to a complex sentence by expanding a word or phrase into a subordinate clause. This clause may be a noun, adjective or adverb clause.

Example: His silence proves his guilt. (simple)
His silence proves that he is guilty. (complex)

D. Rewrite the following sentences as directed, without changing their meanings.

1. He reached the office and began to work. (Begin with 'On…')
____
2. If you work hard, you will not fail. (Remove 'not'.)
____
3. He praised me and rewarded me. (Begin with 'Not only did…')
____
4. He is so clever that he accepted the offer. (Rewrite using 'too'.)
____

5. The poet sat under the tree gazing at the stars. (Use 'and'.)

____

6. Harry closed the door of the chamber and turned to find Snape looking at him. (Begin with 'No sooner…')

____

7. Though they are wealthy, they are hardworking. (Use 'In spite of'.)

____

8. The child woke up with a start and began crying. (Use 'Waking up...')

____

9. The fact that he spoke the truth won him many friends. (Begin with 'Speaking…')

____

10. We must complete the syllabus. We have three chapters left. (Join the sentences. Use 'to')

____

Listening and Speaking

A. Listen to the passage and fill in the blanks using the words in the box.

applause	advance	costumes	bouquets	memorable	spectacular
success	ballet	curtain	performance	thrilling	

My first visit to the Royal Opera House was ____________________. My friend and I had gone to see the famous ____________________ *Swan Lake* by Tchaikovsky. There was a great rush for tickets, so we ensured we had bought ours in ____________________. Our excitement led us to arrive for the show half an hour earlier. At sharp 7, the ____________________ began. The first few moments were ____________________. Everything I saw on the stage deeply impressed me. The ____________________ were fine. The dancing and music were captivating. In my entire life, I had never seen anything more ____________________, so grand in scale. Along with me, my friend also enjoyed every minute of it. When the ____________________ fell at the end of the performance, there came a storm of ____________________. It seemed that it would never end. The dancers were presented with large ____________________ of flowers. We also applauded enthusiastically. The performance was a great ____________________.

B. Dramatising a poem can be great fun and can test the limits of your creativity. Attempt an enactment of the following stanzas from the poem 'The Crocodile' by Lewis Carroll.

How doth the little crocodile
Improve his shining tail,
And pour the waters of the Nile
On every golden scale!

How cheerfully he seems to grin!
How neatly spread his claws,
And welcomes little fishes in
With gently smiling jaws!

C. Now, read the poem 'The Walrus and the Carpenter' by the same poet. Present a dramatised version of it to the class.

Pen it Down

Write a descriptive account about a strange encounter you had with an unknown person that has left a lasting impression on you.

18

Twelfth Night

Way with Words

Archaic Words

Make sentences with the following archaic words.

1. thy

____

2. doth

____

3. hath

____

4. aught

____

5. oft

____

Grammar in Use

Direct and Indirect Speech

When we refer to the exact words of the speaker in a sentence, it is said to be in **direct speech**. When we report what somebody said or thought in our own words, we use **indirect speech**.

You have learnt that when we change a sentence from direct to indirect speech, we change the following.

1. The tense of the verb
2. The reporting verb (*said* → *told*, *asked*) followed by *that*.

3. Personal pronouns, possessive pronouns and possessive adjectives
4. Punctuation marks used
5. Expressions of time and place

Examples: My father said, 'Will you return in time for the party tomorrow?' (direct speech)
My father asked me if I would return in time for the party the next day. (indirect speech)

A. Convert these sentences into indirect speech.

1. 'Be friendly with everyone at your new school,' my mother advised.
2. 'Where have you been all this time?' asked Neera.
3. 'Don't be disrespectful towards your elders,' said Mrs Sen.
4. 'I can't drive a car,' said Timmy.
5. 'I have heard so much about you!' exclaimed Rosie.

B. Convert these sentences into direct speech. Punctuate the sentences.

1. Sohail said that he is leaving the country tonight.
2. Gauri asked me about my parents' health.
3. Mrs Puri said that she was going to visit her parents that weekend.
4. Sonam said that it was the hottest day of June.
5. Atharva asked me where I had bought my sports shoes from.
6. The librarian urged us to be quiet in the library.

C. Convert the following passage into indirect speech.

'What are you going to do about the alien in our cupboard?' asked Sam.

'We can always try to send him away in a spaceship!' piped in little Bertie.

'How can we do that? His spaceship has left him and gone forever!' said Sam.

Norah looked up and smiled as she said, 'Let's call up NASA. Maybe they can help.'

'We can't call up NASA. They might ask too many questions,' said Sam.

'But I really think we should make the call to NASA!' insisted Norah.

Listening and Speaking

A. Imagine that your friend has found your lost wallet. In pairs, write and enact the conversation where you thank your friend for his/her help.

You may use some of the following expressions:

- I really appreciate your help.
- I don't know how to express my gratitude.
- What you've done for me means a lot.
- Thank you from the bottom of my heart for everything.
- How can I possibly thank you?

B. Read these sentences aloud, with emphasis on the underlined words. Write the meaning of the sentence in each case.

1. *Sujata* will never accept her folly.
   Sujata will never accept *her* folly.
   Sujata will *never* accept her folly.
2. Hello, can *I* see your ID?
   Hello, can I see *your* ID?
   Hello, can I see your *ID*?

Pen it Down

A. Your city has recently been affected by a powerful cyclone. Write a newspaper report describing the devastation you have seen around your city.

Include the following in your report:

- the date and time of impact
- safety measures taken by civic authorities
- your personal experience

B. Your school is organising a relief camp for cyclone victims. Make a poster asking your fellow students to make donations. This poster will be displayed on the school notice board.

Include the following in your poster:

- items requested as relief material
- collection point and date

Assessment

Comprehension

Text A. Read the passage and answer the questions that follow. It is an article about the skittering frog, a new species in the world of animal studies.

One of the latest discoveries to cause a ripple in the world of animal studies is that of a new species of the skittering frog. It was identified in the lush surroundings of the Thattekkad Bird Sanctuary in Kerala.

A team of adept researchers from the Zoological Survey of India (ZSI), Mount Carmel College (MCC), Bengaluru, and National Institute of Science Education and Research (NISER), Bhubaneswar, made the discovery. It was a part of the Zoological Survey of India's exploratory and documentation programme on bird species in the Thattekkad Bird Sanctuary. The research findings of the study have been published in an international journal named *Zootaxa*, from New Zealand. It has drawn the attention of the scientific world.

The study is part of a specialised approach wherein scientists utilize the study of the arrangement of the parts of living things, genetic studies and other such guidelines to prove their findings of new species.

Preliminary studies have indicated that this new species might also be located in the freshwater bodies at the foothills of the Western Ghats, south of the Palakkad Gap. Conservation of these freshwater bodies is important for the preservation of this species of frogs. Other frogs in this genus group have been found in regions of the Arabian Peninsula, Pakistan, India, Nepal, Sri Lanka, Myanmar, and Thailand. This new discovery shows that some of the skittering frogs are endemic to India.

As of now, Kerala is known to have 180 species of frogs and there could be many more new species awaiting formal descriptions. The study team says that it took a long time to resolve the problems as the locality names mentioned in the descriptions of historical species were ambiguous which created a sense of perplexity. This prevailed for subsequent findings as well. Use of locality names often obscure the findings of new species for a while till detailed research brings them into the spotlight.

Questions

1. Find and copy the correct words to answer the questions below.

   a. Which term refers to the genus of a frog type? (1 mark)

   ____

b. Where is Mount Carmel College? (1 mark)

c. Which state is known to have 180 species of frogs? (1 mark)

2. Find and copy one word that tells you that the skittering frog species was identified from healthy surroundings. (1 mark)

3. Find and copy the name of two cities that suggest where the team of researchers were from. (1 mark)

4. *Kerala is home to many endemic species of frogs.* – What does the word 'home' mean in this sentence? (2 marks)

5. Explain what preliminary studies have indicated regarding the new species. (1 mark)

6. *The study team says that it took a long time to resolve the problems as the locality names mentioned in the historical species descriptions were ambiguous which created a sense of perplexity.*

   Copy one phrase from the list below that correctly matches the meaning of 'sense of perplexity'.

   sense of fear, sense of confusion, sense of anxiety (1 mark)

7. Why is conservation of freshwater bodies important? (3 marks)

8. Why is the use of locality names a problem? (3 marks)

Text B. Read the passage and answer the questions that follow. It is an extract from the story of Perseus, from the book *Heroes* by Charles Kingsley, where the great Greek hero Perseus meets Medusa, a monstrous figure.

Perseus, son of Zeus, had grown to be a tall lad and a sailor, and went on many sea voyages. He was the most skilful of all in running and wrestling and boxing, and in rowing with the oar, and in all which befits a man.

One day, Perseus wandered into a pleasant wood, and fell asleep. And as he slept, a strange dream came to him. He saw a lady, taller than he, or any mortal man; but beautiful exceedingly, with great grey eyes. And over her shoulder, there was a mighty shield of brass, polished like a mirror.

She held it up and said: 'See here, Perseus; dare you face such a monster as this, and slay it, that I, Athena, may place its head upon this shield?'

And there appeared a face in the mirror, and as Perseus looked on it, his blood ran cold. It was a beautiful woman; but her cheeks were pale as death, her lips were thin and bitter like a snake's, and instead of hair, vipers wreathed about her temples.

Perseus said: 'If there is anything so fierce and foul on earth, it were a noble deed to kill it. Where can I find it?'

The lady smiled and said: 'This is Medusa, the Gorgon, the mother of a monstrous brood.'

Questions

1. Name Perseus' father. (1 mark)

2. What had Perseus grown to be? (2 marks)

3. Find and copy a word made using the suffix *-ful*. (1 mark)

4. Describe the special qualities of Perseus as narrated in the passage. (3 marks)

5. Who was the lady who appeared in Perseus' dream? (1 mark)

6. What terrifying image did she show Perseus? (2 marks)

7. Who was the lady shown in the mirror? (1 mark)

8. *One day, Perseus wandered into a pleasant wood.* – What does 'wood' mean here? (1 mark)

9. What impression do you gather of Perseus from his response, *'If there is anything so fierce and foul on earth, it were a noble deed to kill it. Where can I find it?'* (3 marks)